CISTERCIAN STUDIES SERIES: NUMBER TWO HUNDRED-TWENTY

BENEDICT OF ANIANE
THE EMPEROR'S MONK

ARDO'S *LIFE*

D1715930

Cistercian Studies Series: Number Two Hundred Twenty

Benedict of Aniane
The Emperor's Monk

Ardo's *Life*

Translated by
Allen Cabaniss

Foreword by
Annette Grabowsky and Clemens Radl

CISTERCIAN PUBLICATIONS
Kalamazoo, Michigan

The work of Cistercian Publications
is made possible in part by support from
Western Michigan University
to the
Institute of Cistercian Studies.

Library of Congress Cataloging-in-Publication Data

Ardo.
    [Vita Benedicti. English. Selections]
    Benedict of Aniane : the emperor's monk Ardo's life / translated by
Allen Cabaniss ; foreword by Annette Grabowsky and Clemens Radl.
    p. cm. — (Cistercian studies series ; no. 220)
    Includes index.
    ISBN 978-0-87907-320-6
    1. Benedict, of Aniane, Saint, ca. 750–821.   2. Christian
saints—France—Biography.   I. Cabaniss, Allen, 1911–   II. Title.
III. Series.

BX4700.B35A721325 2008
271'.102—dc22   2008003606

[B]

The Board and Editors of Cistercian Publications
dedicate this book with affection and respect
to the memory of
Patricia Sommerfeldt

TABLE OF CONTENTS

TABLE OF ABBREVIATIONS

EppKa	*Epistolae Karolini aevi.* Berlin 1892.
MGH	Monumenta Germaniae Historia series
Manitius, *Geschichte*	Max Manitius, *Geschichte der lateinischen Literaur des Mittelalters.* Munich: Beck, 1911.
Mühlbacher, *Regesta*	J. Böhmer, E. Mühlbacher, J. Lechner, *Die Regesten des Kaiserreichs unter den Karolingern 751-918.* Innsbruck: Verlag der Wagner'schen Universitäts-Buchhandlung, 1908
PL	J.-P. Migne, *Patrologia cursus completus series Latina*
PLAC	MGH Poetae Latini aevi Carolini
SS	MGH Scriptores
SS rer. Merow	MGH Scriptores rerum Merovingicarum

THE SECOND BENEDICT

A REVIEW OF RECENT SCHOLARSHIP

BENEDICTUS II

Benedictus secundus—'the second Benedict'—is how Benedict of Aniane was reverently referred to soon after his death.[1] This nickname establishes him as the legitimate successor to his famous namesake Benedict of Nursia, whose name to this day is equated with the *Regula Benedicti*, and who is popularly celebrated as the founder of benedictine monasticism. For quite some time, however, historians have realized however, that it was not Benedict of Nursia, but Benedict of Aniane who was in fact the 'organizer of true benedictine monasticism'.[2]

BENEDICT OF NURSIA

We owe all our knowledge of Benedict of Nursia to a single source. Gregory the Great, pope from 590 to 604, devoted to Benedict the second book of his *Dialogues*, a work which in four books describes the 'Lives and Miracles of the Saints in Italy'.[3] Any historian interested in Benedict's biography will find reading this book inevitably disappointing, as the actual facts Gregory delivers on Benedict's life are exceedingly

---

1. *Capitula qualiter observationes sacrae in nonnullis monasteriis habentur quas bonae memoriae Benedictus secundus in coenobiis suis alumnis habere instituit*, ed. by Hieronymus Frank, Corpus Consuetudinum monasticarum 1 (Siegburg: Schmitt, 1963) 353.

2. Josef Semmler, Heinrich Bacht, 'Benedikt von Aniane', in *Lexikon des Mittelalters* 1 (Munich: Artemis, 1980) 1864–1867, here 1864.

3. Gregory the Great, *Dialogues,* ed. by Adalbert de Vogüé (Paris: Éditions du Cerf, 1979) 2:126–248.

sparse. This, as far as we can reconstruct it, is the outline of Benedict's biography. Born in Nursia (Umbria) and from a respected family, he was sent by his parents to school in Rome. To avoid succumbing to the dissolute and licentious lifestyle there, he abandoned his studies and left the city to live as a hermit east of Rome, near Tivoli.[4] His fame as a man of God spread rapidly, and he was soon appointed abbot of a monastery. His strict concept of the regular life, however, antagonized the monks, who proceeded to conspire against him. Benedict survived an attempted poisoning and left to establish a group of twelve monasteries of his own in nearby Subiaco. Encountering hostility there as well, he moved to Casinum (Montecassino), where he destroyed an existing pagan shrine and replaced it with his most famous monastery. There he remained until his death.

The few external historical events (famines, contacts with Goths) that allow an exact dating enable us to narrow Benedict's lifetime down to the years from around 480/490 to 550/560. Available information therefore is anything but profuse.

It was not Gregory's goal, however, to compose a meticulous *curriculum vitae* of the saint. In the words of Karl S. Frank, it is rather an 'interpreted biography'.[5] The four fictitious dialogues between Gregory and his deacon Peter, including the lives of Benedict and forty-nine other Italian saints, were intended to serve as examples for Peter. The miracle stories were intended, not for historical instruction, but for religious edification—a common practice in the Middle Ages. Gregory devotes the second book of these dialogues primarily to the miracles performed by Benedict as a way of portraying Benedict's path toward sainthood.

The hagiographical nature of the narrative is not the only thing to have aroused doubts among historians; even Gregory's authorship has come into question. The British historian Francis Clark argues that Gregory cannot be considered to be the author of the *Dialogues* for a variety of reasons which he explicates in two studies.[6] Clark assumes

---

4. Gregory the Great, *Dialogues* II, Prol. 1; Vogüé, 126.
5. Karl S. Frank, 'Die Benediktusregel und ihre Auslegung bis Benedikt von Aniane', *Rottenburger Jahrbuch für Kirchengeschichte* 9 (1990) 11–25, here 12.
6. Francis Clark, *The Pseudo-Gregorian Dialogues.* 2 volumes (Leiden: Brill, 1987), and recently *idem, The 'Gregorian' Dialogues and the Origins of Benedictine Monasticism* (Leiden: Brill, 2003).

that the *Dialogues* were written by a 'dialogist' towards the end of the seventh century, roughly one hundred years after Gregory's death.

Clark's views have not gained general acceptance, however, and Gregory, by common consent, continues to be credited with the authorship of the *Dialogues*, though some agree that he may not have published them himself.[7] Another line of criticism has been aimed, not at the circumstances of their genesis, but at the very content of the *Dialogue* on Benedict. Johannes Fried recently posed the question: who was Benedict of Nursia? Actually the question should read: did Benedict of Nursia really exist, or was he in reality perhaps nothing more than a 'myth, a pious legend, a phantom'?[8] Provoking this query is the fact that the sole source for Benedict's life was not written down until half a century after his death. Gregory did not know him personally, though he mentions numerous authorities who told him all about Benedict.[9] Yet no further information about these men can be found anywhere. Similarly, we are unable to substantiate the story of Benedict by comparison with another source.

Another point of contention for Fried is the fact that Benedict— supposedly quite famous in his own lifetime—appears to have remained virtually unknown in Italy until the eighth century.[10] In fact, the first traces of his veneration are found in Gaul, not in Italy. According to an ancient tradition, a delegation from the abbey Fleury-sur-Loire was sent to Montecassino in the late seventh century to obtain relics of Benedict and his sister Scholastica for Gaul.[11] In Italy, by contrast, there are no

7. Paul Meyvaert, 'The Enigma of Gregory the Great's Dialogues: A response to Francis Clark', *The Journal of Ecclesiastical History* 39 (1988) 335–381; Pius Engelbert, 'Neue Forschungen zu den "Dialogen" Gregors des Großen. Antworten auf Clarks These', *Erbe und Auftrag* 65 (1989) 376–393; Johannes Fried, 'Gedächtnis in der Kritik: Chlodwigs Taufe und Benedikts Leben', in *idem, Der Schleier der Erinnerung. Grundzüge einer historischen Memorik* (Darmstadt: Wissenschaftliche Buchgesellschaft, 2004) 333–357 and 434–441.
8. Fried, *Gedächtnis in der Kritik*, 356.
9. Gregory the Great, *Dialogues* II, Prol. 1 (Vogüé, 126); see also Kassius Hallinger, 'Papst Gregor der Grosse und der hl. Benedikt', in Basilius Steidle, ed., *Commentationes in regulam S. Benedicti* (Rome: Herder, 1957) 231–320, here 254 f.
10. Fried, *Gedächtnis in der Kritik*, 353 f.
11. Fried, *Gedächtnis in der Kritik*, 354.

signs of veneration: his tomb was neglected, and no one bore his name.[12] Not until the early eighth century did Rome begin to show signs of a certain reverence for Benedict of Nursia, and around 718, under Abbot Petronax, Pope Gregory II set about rebuilding Benedict's monastery at Montecassino, which had been destroyed by the Lombards at the end of the sixth century.[13]

In general, this meager framework of concrete data—amplified by miracle stories and containing very few individual elements, mainly provided by place names—is so vague and unspecific that, theoretically, it could be applied to virtually any founder of any sixth century abbey.[14] The same also applies to the clichéd description of Benedict of Aniane's life.[15]

THE AGE OF THE COMBINED RULE

Veneration for Benedict of Nursia did not begin immediately after his death, nor, as we said, did it begin in Italy. Nor did the rule commonly ascribed to Benedict gain immediate widespread acceptance. Gregory's *Dialogue* contains a brief chapter in which reference is made to a rule reputedly written by Benedict.[16] This rule, however, is characterized merely as a particularly suitable rule for monks; details about its structure or content are not disclosed. Gregory was neither a propagator of the *Regula Benedicti* nor of benedictine monasticism, as this chapter might lead readers to believe. Gregory himself did not observe the benedictine Rule, nor did he implement it in his monastery, Saint Andrew in Rome.[17] Indeed, up until the tenth century there is no evidence of any community in Rome living by this rule.

Contrary to later developments in the Middle Ages, as well as in modern practice, in Gregory's time there was no concept of one single

12. The translation of his remains is currently considered improbable; for a summary see Fried, *Gedächtnis in der Kritik*, 439 f., note 118.

13. Paulus Diaconus, *Historia Langobardorum* VI 40; ed. Georg Waitz, MGH Scriptores rerum Langobardicarum et Italicarum saec. VI–IX (Hannover: Hahn, 1878) 178f.

14. See Fried, *Gedächtnis in der Kritik*, 351.

15. See below: 'The Beginning of Benedict of Aniane's Monastic Career'.

16. Gregory the Great, *Dialogues* II, 36; Vogüé, 242.

17. Hallinger (n. 9 above), 'Papst Gregor der Grosse und der hl. Benedikt'.

rule characteristic of a specific order and distinguishing it from others. There were no monastic orders, one did not live as a 'Benedictine' or as a 'Pachomian'; one chose a specific lifestyle: anchorite, cenobite, or itinerant monk.[18] When composing a rule for his community, the founder of a monastery not uncommonly drew from existing rules, and combined this material with new elements meeting the specific requirements of his community. Benedict of Nursia was no exception. His rule, for example, corresponds strongly to and is probably dependent on the *Regula Magistri,* whose author to this day remains anonymous.[19] Benedict's Rule, therefore, is not an original work: it was eclectic, as were all others at the time. To be absolutely accurate, one really should not refer to Benedict of Nursia as 'the father of Western monasticism'![20] According to the final chapter of the *Regula Benedict,* not even Benedict himself claimed exclusivity for his Rule. He regarded it as a 'little rule for beginners'. Those who were seeking perfection were encouraged to abide by the Bible and the writings of the Fathers, such as Cassian and Basil.[21]

In accordance with the custom of the times, therefore, the *Regula Benedicti* was combined with other rules and not implemented exclusively—except perhaps at Montecassino. Thus we refer to this period before the *Regula Benedicti* was declared the sole valid rule for all monastic communities as the 'Age of the Combined Rule'.

The first signs of the diffusion of Benedict's Rule may be observed in southern Gaul. In a letter dating from around 620/630, an abbot named Venerandus announces to Bishop Constantius of Albi that he has implemented *regulam sancti Benedicti abbatis Romensis* in Altaripa.[22] Noteworthy is the reference to Benedict as a roman abbot—apparently Venerandus

18. Compare, for example, the famous chapter in the Rule on the different types of monks: *Regula Benedicti* 1; ed. Rudolf Hanslik (Wien: Hoelder-Pichler-Tempsky, ²1977) 18–20, and Hallinger, 'Papst Gregor der Grosse und der hl. Benedikt', 259.

19. See the summary provided by David Knowles, 'The *Regula Magistri* and the Rule of St Benedict', in Knowles, *Great Historical Enterprises. Problems in Monastic History* (London: Nelson, 1963) 135–195.

20. Cf. Bernd Jaspert, 'Benedikt von Nursia–der Vater des Abendlandes? Kritische Bemerkungen zur Typologie eines Heiligen', *Erbe und Auftrag* 49 (1973) 90–103 and 190–207.

21. *Regula Benedicti* 73; Hanslik, 179–181.

22. Ludwig Traube, *Textgeschichte der Regula S. Benedicti* (Munich: Franz, ²1910) 87 f.; Friedrich Prinz, *Frühes Mönchtum im Frankenreich. Kultur und Gesellschaft in*

had no knowledge of Gregory the Great's *Vita Benedicti*. The oldest testimony for the observance of the *Regula Benedicti* in combination with
other rules occurs in the rule which Bishop Donatus of Besançon, a
student of the renowned monk Columbanus, compiled for his monastery
of women between 630 and 635. The greatest portion of this combined
rule consists of forty-three chapters from the Rule of Benedict.[23]

Up until well into the eighth century, the Rule of Benedict was
dispersed by means of combined rules of this kind, mainly in combination with the Irish Rule of Columbanus. The dispersion of this rule-
combination occurred within the context of the spread of iro-frankish
monasticism from Luxeuil Abbey, its center in the Vosgues Mountains.[24]
From the seventh century on, exclusive observance of the Rule of
Benedict became gradually more common, thanks to the initiative of
anglo-saxon monasticism. By then, the Rule was generally perceived
as the work of a roman abbot, a claim which seems to have recommended it to the Anglo-Saxons, who were close associates of Rome.[25]
Willibrord and especially Boniface endorsed the *Regula Benedicti* and
established its exclusive observance in the monasteries they founded
on the continent, as at Fulda Abbey in 744.[26] Prior to that, in 742,
Boniface had decreed at his first synod, the *Concilium Germanicum*, that
all monks and nuns were to live exclusively according to the *Regula
Benedicti*. We know however, that not all communities considered this
binding.[27]

*Gallien, den Rheinlanden und Bayern am Beispiel der monastischen Entwicklung (4. bis 8.
Jahrhundert)* (Darmstadt: Wissenschaftliche Buchgesellschaft, ²1988) 267f.

23. Prinz, *Frühes Mönchtum*, 285; Michaela Zelzer, 'Die Regula Donati, der älteste Textzeuge der Regula Benedicti', *Regulae Benedicti Studia* 16 (1989) 23–36.

24. Examples may be found in: Prinz, *Frühes Mönchtum*, 272–289.

25. Regarding the alleged roman origin of the Rule see: Pius Engelbert, 'Regeltext und Romverehrung. Zur Frage der Regula Benedicti im Frühmittelalter',
Römische Quartalschrift für christliche Altertumskunde und Kirchengeschichte 81 (1986)
39–60.

26. Bonifatius, ep. 86; ed. Michael Tangl, *Die Briefe des Heiligen Bonifatius und
Lullus,* MGH Epistolae selectae 1 (Berlin: Weidmann, 1916) 193, line 20.

27. *Concilium Germanicum* c. 7; ed. Albert Werminghoff, MGH Concilia aevi
Karolini 1 (Hannover: Hahn, 1906) 4. See also Wilfried Hartmann, *Die Synoden der
Karolingerzeit im Frankenreich und in Italien* (Paderborn: Schöningh, 1989) 50–53;
Josef Semmler, 'Benedictus II: una regula—una consuetudo', in Willem Lourdaux,

The anglo-saxon reformers received substantial support from the Carolingians, who had maintained close relations with the popes in Rome since the reign of Pepin III, Charlemagne's father. Since the popes were actively endorsing benedictine monasticism by the first decades of the eighth century—by rebuilding Montecassino for instance—the Carolingians acknowledged Rome's preferred Rule and strove to implement it politically as well. As Rome was deemed the repository of authentic tradition, it was the natural place to consult in looking for a copy of the Rule of Benedict. In 787 Charlemagne went on a mission to Benedict's own domain in Montecassino and, shortly thereafter, he ordered a transcript to be made of the copy of the Rule there. This copy, alleged to have been written by Benedict himself, had supposedly been taken to Rome by monks fleeing the abbey after its destruction by the Lombards,[28] and then restored to Montecassino by Pope Zachary in the 740s. Charlemagne declared this transcript of the Montecassino copy the model text and the obligatory monastic Rule for his entire empire.[29] Reminders to observe the Benedictine Rule were issued regularly at several synods: in 802 at Aachen and at the reform synods in 813, but it was apparently difficult to convince the monastic communities to relinquish their accustomed constitutions.[30]

The eventual dominance of the Rule of Benedict did not necessarily mean that all earlier monastic traditions were entirely abandoned. This is manifested by the great variety of rules present in the great monastic libraries of the ninth century. On their shelves the rules of

---

Daniël Verhelst, edd., *Benedictine Culture 750–1050* (Leuven: Leuven University Press, 1983) 1–49, here 3f.

28. *Epistula ad regem Karolum de monasterio sancti Benedicti directa et a Paulo dictata*, ed. Kassius Hallinger, Maria Wegener, *Corpus consuetudinum monasticarum* 1 (Siegburg: Schmitt, 1963) 157–175, here 159 f. See also Rudolf Schieffer, '"Redeamus ad fontem"'. Rom als Hort authentischer Überlieferung im frühen Mittelalter', *Roma—Caput et Fons. Zwei Vorträge über das päpstliche Rom zwischen Altertum und Mittelalter* (Opladen: Westdeutscher Verlag, 1989) 45–70, here 62.

29. Charlemagne's copy is not preserved in the original. A transcription is extant at Saint Gall Abbey. Studies have shown, however, that Charlemagne's model text did not gain general acceptance. Other independent versions of the *Regula Benedicti* were more popular: Klaus Zelzer, 'Zur Stellung des Textus receptus und des interpolierten Textes in der Textgeschichte der Regula S. Benedicti', *Revue bénédictine* 88 (1978) 205–246.

30. Semmler, 'Benedictus II', 4f.; Oexle, Forschungen 112f., 112–133.

Basil, Columbanus and Benedict rested side-by-side.[31] This was quite
in accordance with the spirit of the last chapter of Benedict's rule, which
encourages the reading of the writings of the Fathers. Benedict of
Aniane's *Concordia regularum* was in essence compiled with similar intent,
not to propagate the exclusivity of the *Regula Benedicti,* but to manifest
its harmonious accord with other rules just as valuable and worthy of
study.[32]

THE BEGINNING OF BENEDICT OF ANIANE'S MONASTIC CAREER

As the *Regula Benedicti* embarked on its triumphal march through the
Frankish Empire, Benedict of Aniane, at the beginning of his monastic
career on the empire's periphery, appears to have been committed to
the combined-rule tradition. Still in royal service, he could practice
asceticism only covertly after his conversion. Entering a monastery was
not his first choice, and he was uncertain about which form of religious
life he should choose (*Life* 1.2). After his brother's tragic accident—the
incident which provoked his change of life—he secretly entered the
monastery of Saint Seine, near Dijon. This may have occurred at the
advice of a monk named Widmar, whom he consulted for guidance
(2.2). At this point, he was still far removed from the idea of *una regula*.
He also does not appear to have been ideally suited to communal life.
His form of asceticism was so severe that it proved to be incompatible
with community life, and he essentially lived as an anchorite among
cenobites. His individuality, not entirely devoid of egoism, prompted
the abbot to intervene and remind Benedict to abide by the *Regula
Benedicti.* This was nothing more than a rule 'for beginners and weak
persons' in Benedict's mind, who much preferred the rules of Basil and
Pachomius (2.5). Though living in a monastic community observing
the Rule of Benedict, he himself apparently lived by the code of some

31. Prinz, *Frühes Mönchtum*, 290, with examples.
32. Pierre Bonnerue, 'Introduction', in Ardon, *Vie de Benoît d'Aniane*, translated
by Fernand Baumes (Bégrolles en Mauges: Abbaye de Bellefontaine, 2001) 17–43,
here 40f.; Semmler, 'Benedictus II', 27; voicing views similar to those of Bonnerue:
Adalbert de Vogüé, 'La Concordia regularum de Benoît d'Aniane: son vrai but et sa
structure', in Giovanni Spinelli, ed., *Il monachesimo italiano dall'età longobarda all'età
ottoniana (secc. VIIX)* (Cesena: Badia di Santa Maria del Monte, 2006) 39–45.

combined rule, albeit an unwritten one. Suddenly, Benedict began to demonstrate enthusiasm for the *Regula Benedicti* (2.5). This change of heart transformed him in the eyes of his brethren from a ridiculed misfit to an integrated member of the community, a process concluded by his promotion to the office of cellarer (2.6). During this time, he fully assimilated the *Regula Benedicti* and was even elected abbot. He fled from this office, however, realizing that his uncompromising lifestyle was incompatible with that of the brothers. He withdrew to his home and, together with Widmar and others sympathetic to his ideas, he established on his father's land near the small river Aniane a monastic settlement of his own, a *cella exigua* (3.1).

We are unable to judge how much of this narrative is true to fact, especially the description of Benedict's excessive asceticism. The limited information at Ardo's disposal (Preface: b, 42), leads us strongly to suspect that, in many passages, he simply used his imagination or reverted to literary modes or *topoi*. The parallels to Benedict of Nursia's *Vita* are pronounced. The basic framework of the stations of his life applies to Benedict of Aniane's equally well. The early circumstances are similar: both are of noble birth and sent away for their education (Rome / Aachen). Both take their first steps in religious life as anchorites, until they are taken on by monks (Romanus / Widmar). Both experience a period of failure before establishing their own monasteries. Both are elected abbot and both reject the office for the same reason: that their lifestyles were divergent from those of their brethren (*moribus non convenire*).[33] The correspondences go beyond mere content; in part even the phrasing of Ardo's *Vita* follows Gregory's *Vita Benedicti*. From the first chapter, it should have been instantly clear to every medieval reader of the *Life* that Benedict of Aniane stood firmly in the tradition of his namesake, that he was a *Benedictus secundus*. *Vir venerabilis nomine et merito Benedictus* is but a slight variation of the opening sentence of Gregory the Great's second book of the *Dialogues* that comments on Benedict's speaking name.[34]

---

33. Regarding these parallels see: Josef Narberhaus, *Benedikt von Aniane. Werk und Persönlichkeit* (Münster: Aschendorff, 1930) 11f.

34. Gregory's second book of the *Dialogues* begins: *Fuit uir uitae uenerabilis, gratia Benedictus et nomine* (*Regula Benedicti* Prol. 1; Hanslik, 126); regarding Benedict's name 'Witiza', see Cabaniss' Introduction, p. 36 below.

BENEDICT OF ANIANE AND THE RESOLUTIONS OF AACHEN

Benedict of Aniane is commonly portrayed as a figure inseparable from the monastic reforms of Aachen promulgated in the second decade of the ninth century. There appears to be no doubt about his participation: Ardo reports that after Louis the Pious invested Benedict with general authority over all monasteries of the empire, Benedict met with many abbots and monks, and together they compiled a set of prescriptions which he then presented to the emperor for ratification (36.1). Benedict's relationship to Louis the Pious is mentioned repeatedly in the *Life*. They were in contact during Louis' reign in Aquitaine, where the king commissioned the abbot to reform the religious houses in this province (29.1).[35] This close relationship is confirmed by a donation charter for Aniane Abbey dating from around 808, which historians have long overlooked.[36] Louis' interest in Benedict's work did not subside when he succeeded his father Charlemagne in 814. First he summoned the abbot to the alsatian abbey of Marmoutier, then to Inden, closer to Aachen, to establish a monastery there (35.1-2).[37] According to Ardo, Louis also invested Benedict with general authority over all the monasteries of the empire (36.1). This position did not entail the authority of a modern 'Abbot General'; instead, as historians stress with reference to other prominent coeval abbots and bishops, Benedict's role was more that of a co-coordinator than of a 'super abbot'.[38]

35. See also: Semmler, 'Benedictus II', 7–9; *idem*, 'Benediktinische Reform und kaiserliches Privileg. Zur Frage des institutionellen Zusammenschlusses der Klöster um Benedikt von Aniane', in Gerd Melville, ed., *Institutionen und Geschichte. Theoretische Aspekte und mittelalterliche Befunde* (Cologne: Böhlau, 1992) 259–293, here 271–274.

36. Mark Mersiowsky was the first to draw attention to this charter; see Mark Mersiowsky, 'Zur Edition der Diplome Ludwigs des Frommen', in Ellen Widder *et al.*, edd., *Manipulus Florum* (Münster: Waxmann, 2000) 307–340, here 323–330.

37. The Moissac Chronicle also records this incident: *Chronicon Moissiacense* ad 814, ed. Georg Heinrich Pertz, MGH Scriptores 1 (Hannover: Hahn, 1826) 311, lines 27–31.

38. Semmler, 'Benediktinische Reform und kaiserliches Privileg', 276 f. and 289 note 226; Dieter Geuenich, 'Kritische Anmerkungen zur sogenannten "anianischen Reform"', in Dieter R. Bauer *et al.*, edd., *Mönchtum—Kirche—Herrschaft 750–1000* (Sigmaringen: Thorbecke, 1998) 99–112, here 102/103; Mayke De Jong, 'Carolingian Monasticism: The Power of Prayer', in Rosamond McKitterick,

In order to extend the reforms implemented in his kingdom of Aquitaine to all religious houses of the empire in the course of his *renovatio regni Francorum*, Louis convened two synods for the purpose of directing his program towards appropriate legislation. The main goal of these two synods, convened in August 816 and July 817, was to divide the religious communities into two distinctive groups: all monastic communities were to receive the same constitution (the *una consuetudo*), while establishments of canons and canonesses, as well as all other non-monastic religious houses, were to receive a separate rule of their own. While the sources documenting the canonical reform are quite plentiful, remarkably, the written sources from these synods pertaining to the monastic reform are not only exceedingly scarce, but rather complicated as well.[39] The only extant legislative sources for the monastic reform are:

1. For the 816 synod there are the texts historians refer to as the *acta praeliminaria*: a) the 'Statuta Murbacensia' from the alsatian abbey of Murbach, a transcription of the topics of the proceedings, recorded before the close of the hearings and just possibly extant in the original; b) a capitular text that also appears to be a private recording of the council resolutions ('*Praeliminarium* of Rouen').[40] In addition, a capitulary of Louis the Pious is preserved in three manuscripts dating from the ninth and twelfth centuries.[41]

---

ed., *The New Cambridge Medieval History* 2: *C. 700–c. 900* (Cambridge: Cambridge University Press, 1995) 681–694, here 632.

39. A survey of the extant manuscripts may be found in: Hubert Mordek, *Bibliotheca capitularium regum Francorum manuscripta. Überlieferung und Traditionszusammenhang der fränkischen Herrschererlasse,* MGH Hilfsmittel 15 (Munich: MGH, 1995) 1045–1058.

40. *Actuum praeliminarium Synodi primae Aquisgranensis commentationes sive Statua Murbacensia,* ed. by Semmler, Corpus Consuetudinum monasticarum 1:441–450; *Synodi primae Aquisgranensis acta praeliminaria,* ed. Semmler, Corpus Consuetudinum monasticarum 1:435–436; Semmler, 'Zur Überlieferung der monastischen Gesetzgebung Ludwigs des Frommen', *Deutsches Archiv für Erforschung des Mittelalters* 16 (1960) 309–388, here 321–332.

41. *Synodi primae Aquisgranensis decreta authentica;* Semmler, *Corpus Consuetudinum monasticarum* 1, 457–468; referred to as 'Capitulare monasticum I' in Mordek, *Bibliotheca capitularium*, 999–1005; Semmler, 'Zur Überlieferung der monastischen Gesetzgebung', 332–337; regarding the synod see: Josef Semmler, 'Die Beschlüsse

2. The result of the proceedings of July 817, preserved only in one of Louis' capitularies and comprising forty-three chapters, is found in a twelfth-century manuscript (two early modern printed versions reproduce the text of two manuscripts, now lost).[42]

3. Another document bearing the same date as the 817 capitulary was published by Josef Semmler under the title *Regula Sancti Benedicti Abbatis Anianensis sive collectio capitularis*, and dated by him to 818/819.[43] This capitulary contains no new material, but rather combines the decrees of 816 and 817. In view of the great number of manuscripts reproducing this document, as well as their dates (ninth to fifteenth centuries), it appears that this document was considered throughout the Middle Ages to have been the central source for the Aachen decrees. The puzzling date of the document does raise some questions. Indubitably, however, a great assembly of abbots and monks convened in Aachen on 10 July 817. But why publish two different versions of the decrees—a shorter one *and* a longer one that contains the shorter one plus the 816 capitulary—as the result of one and the same synod?

The Frankish Royal Annals—amazingly—do not record the monastic reforms until the year 818; the assemblies of 816 and 817 are not mentioned there: After Christmas 818, a synod took place in Aachen; there many matters pertaining to the church and monasticism were discussed.[44] Chapter Five of the *Capitulare ecclesiasticum* enacted at this occasion includes some monastic legislation. Among other prescriptions, it upholds the monastic lifestyle as previously recorded in a *scaedula*.[45]

des Aachener Konzils im Jahre 816', *Zeitschrift für Kirchengeschichte* 74 (1963), 15–82.

42. *Synodi secundae Aquisgranensis decreta authentica*, ed. Semmler, Corpus Consuetudinum monasticarum 1:473–481; referred to as 'Capitulare monasticum II' in Mordek, *Bibliotheca capitularium*, 1005–1009. See also Semmler, 'Zur Überlieferung der monastischen Gesetzgebung', 337–341.

43. Corpus Consuetudinum monasticarum 1:515–536; see Semmler, 'Zur Überlieferung der monastischen Gesetzgebung', 341–369.

44. *Annales regni Francorum* ad 819; ed. Friedrich Kurze, MGH Scriptores rerum Germanicarum in usum scholarum separatim editi 6 (Hannover: Hahn, 1895) 150.

45. *Capitulare ecclesiasticum 818/819* c. 5; ed. Alfred Boretius, MGH Capitularia regum Francorum 1 (Hannover: Hahn, 1883) 276, lines 24–28.

The *scaedula* in question might have been the *Collectio capitularis.*[46] If this more extensive, combined capitulary does indeed date from 818/819, it seems somewhat incredible that the legislators did not bother to adjust the date of the synod (all documents carry the date 10 July 817).

4. Another product of the Aachen reforms is the *Notita de servitio monasteriorum*, a list of all taxes and fees the abbeys allegedly owed to the emperor. Its actual relevance to the reform is a matter of dispute.[47]

Other historiographical sources mention the Aachen decrees, but those of 817 and not those of 816. Both the *Chronicon Laurissense breve* and the 'Chronicle of Moissac' state that the assembly of Aachen prescribed the mandatory observance of the *Regula Benedicti* for all monks, and also instigated separate prescriptions for canons.[48] Aside from imposing the observance of the Benedictine Rule *(una regula)*, the synods were also instrumental in establishing *consuetudines*, contemporary regulations that supplemented the Rule, interpreted it, or sometimes even contradicted it.[49] The volumes mentioned here in fact contain these *consuetudines*.

The great accomplishment of the decrees of Aachen was to establish for the first time in history a purely benedictine observance. This brought to an end the age of the combined rule. Henceforth, a Benedictine was someone who, in the spirit of *una regula—una consuetudo*, observed these decrees in his monastic community.[50] Louis did not leave the implementation and observance of the *una consuetudo* up to the

---

46. For the dating of the *Collectio capitularis* see: Semmler, 'Zur Überlieferung der monastischen Gesetzgebung', 361–365.

47. *Notitia de servitio monasteriorum*, ed. Peter Becker, Corpus Consuetudinum monasticarum 1:493–499. The newest study is the still-to-be-published dissertation by Walter Kettemann, Subsidia Anianensia. Überlieferungs- und textgeschichtliche Untersuchungen zur Geschichte Witiza-Benedikts, seines Klosters Aniane und zur sogenannten 'anianischen Reform'. Mit kommentierten Editionen der Vita Benedicti Anianensis, Notitia de servitio monasteriorum, des Chronicon Moissiacense/ Anianense sowie zweier Lokaltraditionen aus Aniane (Gerhard-Mercator-Universität Duisburg, 1999); see also: Geuenich, 'Kritische Anmerkungen', 106–108.

48. *Chronicon Laurissense breve* ad 816, ed. Georg Heinrich Pertz, MGH Scriptores 1 (Hannover: Hahn, 1826) 122, lines 27–33; *Chronicon Moissacense* ad 815; ed. Pertz, 311, lines 40–45.

49. Semmler, 'Benedictus II', 30–47.

50. Semmler, 'Die Beschlüsse des Aachener Konzils', 75f.

monasteries, however, but commissioned *missi* to monitor the effectuation of the decrees.[51] It appears to have been difficult for the abbeys to relinquish their non-benedictine traditions, however. The sources show that numerous abbeys, even prominent communities, were unwilling to do so and chose instead to follow the canonical code.[52] The Aachen reforms were thus only partially successful: the *Regula Benedicti* had triumphed at last, a uniform customary (*consuetudo*), however, remained beyond reach.

Benedict of Aniane's exact role in the Aachen reforms cannot be explicitly gleaned from the official documents recording the results of the synods. It is frustrating that we are not even able to identify all participants by name.[53] And, what is more, we also learn nothing of Benedict of Aniane's participation. Furthermore, there is no mention anywhere in these documents of Benedict's authorship. Little more is to be garnered from the historiographical sources, for that matter: the *Chronicon Moissiacense* records Benedict's summons to Inden, the so-called Astronomus relates only Louis' reform mandate; nor is anything to be learned about Benedict's share in the Aachen reforms from Ermoldus Nigellus.[54] The only one who offers any detail is Ardo, who devotes chapters Thirty-six to Thirty-eight of his *Life* to Benedict's efforts at attaining *una regula* and, especially, *una consuetudo*: 'He ordered many things in conformity with the Rule. But there are a great many matters demanded in daily practice about which the Rule is silent. . . . For the sake of unity and concord or perhaps for the sake of honorable appearance or even out of consideration for human frailty, Benedict commanded some matters that are not inculcated in the Rule. . . . Where a page of the Rule explains less lucidly or remains altogether silent on a matter, he established and supplied with reason and aptness some matters on which, with divine help, I will touch briefly. . . .' (37). Aside from the *Life*, therefore, there is little support from the extant

---

51. Semmler, 'Benediktinische Reform und kaiserliches Privileg', 276f.

52. For examples see: Semmler, 'Benedictus II', 11–18.

53. For the 816 synod see: Hartmann, *Synoden der Karolingerzeit*, 157.

54. *Chronicon Moissiacense* ad 814; ed. Pertz, 311, lines 27–31. Astronomus, *Das Leben Kaiser Ludwigs*, ed. Ernst Tremp, MGH Scriptores rerum Germanicarum in usum scholarum separatim editi 64 (Hannover: Hahn, 1995) 376, lines 10–16. Ermold le Noir, *Poème sur Louis le Pieux et Épitres au roi Pépin*, ed. Edmond Paral (Paris: Les Belles Lettres, 1964) 92–94, verses 1184–1212.

source material for the notion that the 816 and 817 decrees were conceived 'under the decisive influence of the septimanian reformer'.[55]

German scholars have therefore begun to question the legitimacy of the term 'anianian reform'—a term that has never been widespread in anglo-saxon research, where the more appropriate term 'monastic reform' is used. Aniane was of relevance to the reform politics only as long as Benedict resided there. After the emperor called him away, the abbey declined into insignificance. The reform was enacted where Benedict was, so the term 'anianian' is inapplicable.[56]

Reference is also frequently made to the fact that Benedict was not the only reformer of his time. Other distinguished abbots—such as Hilduin of Saint-Denis or Benedict's friend Helisacher—and several bishops also had their share in the reforms. If they had been equally 'fortunate' in receiving a *vita*, we might be compelled to regard the whole monastic reform from an entirely different perspective. What is more, other reforms, some even before 814, had also been undertaken—for example those of Leidrad of Lyon.[57] Beyond dispute, however, is Benedict's role towards an exclusive observance of the *Regula Benedicti*. He was the chief promoter and propagator of this concept.

THE LIFE OF BENEDICT

In the preceding considerations frequent reference has been made to the *Life* of Benedict of Aniane, presented here in english translation. It is the primary source for his career as abbot of Aniane as well as for his political activities in the cause of monastic reform. In the broader perspective of monastic life in the early Middle Ages, and the formation and growth of monasteries, often under adverse circumstances, Ardo's *Life* conveys numerous other points worthy of discussion and further deliberation. It is therefore more than appropriate to take a close look at the source itself. How was the *Life of Benedict* dispersed? What do we know of the evolution of the text and its reliability? And finally, what can be said of its author, Ardo of Aniane?

In the following discussion, the points already explored by Allen Cabaniss in his Introduction, will not be reiterated. Instead we will

55. Semmler, 'Benediktinische Reform und kaiserliches Privileg', 273f.
56. Geuenich, 'Kritische Anmerkungen', 102f.
57. Geuenich, 'Kritische Anmerkungen', 103f.; Oexle, Forschungen, 146–157.

review recent developments or look at new focuses of interest or considerations currently under discussion. The synoptical nature of this introduction and limitations in space prohibit a detailed analysis. The dispersion of the *Life of Benedict* is quite meager.[58] Not one remotely coeval version of the text has survived. The only medieval manuscript containing the *Life* dates from the first half of the twelfth century. That manuscript, the cartulary of Aniane, is now preserved in the departmental archives of Montpellier.[59] When compiling their cartulary, the monks placed Benedict's *Life* at the beginning of the codex; numerous charters relating to the abbey's history follow. The version of the biography found in the cartulary of Aniane corresponds in essence to the one the translation in this edition is based upon.

Upon closer examination, however, the situation is not as simple as it might appear, for the more recent versions of the text show peculiarities that warrant discussion. These versions do not appear in any medieval manuscript, but exist only in modern transcriptions and prints. The first printed version of the *Life* was published by Hugo Ménard in 1638.[60] He published only the preface and chapters 1 to 18.2 and 30 to 44; the portion containing chapters 18.3 to 29 is missing from this edition. It is possible, of course, that Ménard printed an abridged version of the *Life*, but it is puzzling that he makes no mention of the fact.[61] The question arises therefore, whether Ménard might not have had at his disposal some other medieval manuscript containing a different version of the *Vita* not dependant on the cartulary. Furthermore, a letter

58. A list of the manuscripts may be found in Corpus Consuetudinum monasticarum 1:308f. The following is for the most part a summary of Bonnerue, 'Introduction', 22–28.

59. Archives départementales de l'Hérault, Montpellier, 1 H 1. The cartulary's text has been printed, but without commentary or the paleographical, codicological and diplomatic analysis of a critical edition, by Léon Cassan and Edmond Meynial, edd., *Cartulaires des Abbayes d'Aniane et de Gellone publiés d'après les manuscrits originaux: Cartulaire d'Aniane* (Montpellier: Jean Martel Aîné, 1900). Cf. Mersiowsky, 'Zur Edition', 324f.

60. Hugo Ménard, *Concordia regularum auctore S. Benedicto Anianae abbate* (Paris 1638) 1–45.

61. It was not entirely unusual practice for the publishers of early printed editions to abridge the contents of medieval manuscripts without proper documentation. Pierre Bonnerue considers it quite unlikely, however, that Ménard did so in the case of the Benedict *Vita*; cf. Bonnerue, 'Introduction', 23.

dating from 1650 is preserved[62] that comments on the discrepancies between Ménard's printed edition and the longer version found in the cartulary of Aniane. Other letters dating from the seventeenth century reproduce either the shorter version printed by Ménard or precisely those passages missing in his edition.[63] Later prints and editions render the capitulary text or reproduce Ménard's, divulging no information on further manuscripts.

The evidence from the sources described above allows for two feasible explanations. Either Ménard actually did use a medieval manuscript, now lost, that contained an abridged version of the *Life,* and, if so, that the short version originates from Ardo cannot be ruled out entirely. It is also conceivable, of course, that Ménard himself, or the newer source he used, independently abridged the cartulary text. In this case, we would have to continue to assume that the long version was essentially written by Ardo himself.

To resolve this question, comprehensive research is necessary that cannot be accomplished within the scope of this introduction. Firstly, comparative studies of the individual transcriptions, letters, and printed versions are necessary to identify differences and similarities, as well as possible interdependencies. This would necessarily include an analysis of the text itself: the complete *Vita* would need to be scrutinized for coherence; discontinuities would need to be identified and analyzed; the style of the text indubitably ascribed to Ardo would have to be minutely compared to the dubious portions; and finally, the possible motives for text abridgement or revision would need to be explored. In his introduction to a french translation of the *Vita,* Pierre Bonnerue made a first attempt at tackling this task. The summary of the text and manuscript tradition, given above, is based on his study. Bonnerue presents noteworthy arguments to support his hypothesis that the shorter version printed by Ménard in fact represents the older, original version. In his judgment, the crucial revisions to Ardo's text were not made until two hundred years after the fact, sometime during the eleventh century.[64]

---

62. A letter from Michel Moisnel to Dom Claude Chanteloup dated 8 May 1650 (Paris, Bibliothèque nationale de France, lat. 11761, fol. 89–105).

63. For details see: Bonnerue, 'Introduction', 24–26.

64. Bonnerue, 'Introduction', 28–36.

In order to be able better to understand the context behind this
theory, we need briefly to review the history of Aniane Abbey, and to
focus especially on its relationship to the neighboring abbey of Gellone,
also mentioned in the *Life*. Chapter Thirty relates in some detail the
career of the influential and well-known Count William of Toulouse,
who might even have been related in some way to the ruling Carolingian dynasty. In the early ninth century, after retreating from military
and political life, William established the monastery Gellone (today
Saint-Guilhem-du-Désert) near Aniane, and spent the final years of his
life there.[65] Gellone, initially closely associated with Aniane, soon pros-
pered and flourished, becoming a large and prestigious abbey in its own
right. Aniane, on the other hand, declined soon after Benedict's death.
Beyond losing its prominence in Aquitaine, it even lost its independence
intermittently and was beset by grave financial distress. After the mid-
eleventh century, a tedious and fierce dispute developed between the
former sister-houses regarding Gellone's independence.[66] The incident
that presumably precipitated the altercation occurred in 1066, when
the monks of Gellone elected their own abbot without previously

65. For an account on William of Gellone, see the Introduction by Allen
Cabaniss, who also summarizes Arthur J. Zuckerman's theories in *A Jewish Princedom
in Feudal France 768–900* (New York: Columbia University Press, 1972)—which
scholars have widely rejected. See Allen Cabaniss' list of reviews, as well the review by Wilfried Hartmann, *Deutsches Archiv für Erforschung des Mittelalters* 29 (1973)
284f. The most recent studies on William are Philippe Depreux, *Prosopographie de
l'entourage de Louis le Pieux (781–840)* (Sigmaringen: Thorbecke, 1997) 224 f.; Jean-
Loup Lemaître and Daniel Le Blévec, *Le livre du chapitre de Saint-Guilhem-le-Désert*,
ed. Jean Favier (Paris: Académie des Inscriptions et Belles-Lettres, 2004) 24–39; and
Joachim Wollasch, 'Eine adlige Familie des frühen Mittelalters: Ihr Selbstverständnis
und ihre Wirklichkeit', *Archiv für Kulturgeschichte* 39 (1957) 150–188.
66. The most recent findings on the dispute between Aniane and Gellone are
presented by Pierre Chastang, 'Mémoire des moines et mémoire des chanoines:
Réforme, production textuelle et référence au passé carolingien en Bas-Languedoc
(XIe–XIIe siècles)', in Jean-Marie Sansterre, ed., *L'autorité du passé dans les sociétés
médiévales* (Brussels-Rome: Institut Historique Belge de Rome, 2004) 177–202,
see especially 179–188. Still valuable because of its thoroughness, but in many
respects outdated is Wilhelm Pückert, *Aniane und Gellone: Diplomatisch-kritische
Untersuchungen zur Geschichte der Reformen des Benedictinerordens im IX. und X. Jahr-
hundert* (Leipzig: Hinrich'sche Buchhandlung, 1899), and Pierre Tisset, *L'Abbaye de
Gellone au diocèse de Lodève des origines au XIIIe siècle* (Paris: Recueil Sirey, 1933). On
Pückert, see Mersiowsky, 'Zur Edition', 324.

consulting Aniane. The abbot of Aniane appealed to Pope Alexander II with a letter of complaint. While the further development of the dispute remains irrelevant to this discussion, Aniane was defeated in the end. In subsequent decades, the popes repeatedly adjudicated in favor of Gellone's independence.

One of the measures both sides took in the course of their quarrel was the creation of cartularies in which they collected, falsified, or completely forged charters to document their respective former estates and to underscore claims against the opponent or to ward off the other's claims.[67] The *Life of Benedict*, planted in the most prominent position of Aniane's cartulary, falls therefore under the suspicion of having been altered in the course of the conflict. Bonnerue claims to recognize a reaction to Chapter Thirty of the *Life* especially in Chapters Nineteen to Twenty-nine (in his opinion later additions). It would exceed the scope of this introduction to discuss Bonnerue's theory in full detail.[68] We shall, however, at least cite the most important theses of his argument.[69] According to Bonnerue, a careful reading reveals that the chapters in question serve mainly to exalt Aniane with respect to the neighboring abbey. Chapters Nineteen to Twenty-two were designed to reproduce Chapter Thirty in order to demonstrate that Benedict and William possessed the exact same virtues (more strongly pronounced, naturally, in the case of Benedict). The account in Chapter Twenty of Benedict's participation in the council at Arles in 813 disrupts the chronology of the *Vita,* as the events between 792 and 813 are not

---

67. On the Aniane cartulary, see above, note 59. The Gellone cartulary is also available in a printed (but not critical) edition: Paul Alaus, Léon Cassan, Edmond Meynial, edd., *Cartulaires des Abbayes d'Aniane et de Gellone publiés d'après les manuscrits originaux: Cartulaire de Gellone* (Montpellier: Jean Martel Ainé, 1898).
68. A thorough study, to include an analysis of the Benedict *Vita,* has been announced for some time by W. Kettemann. See Walter Kettemann, 'Subsidia Anianensia. Überlieferungs- und textgeschichtliche Untersuchungen zur Geschichte Witiza-Benedikts, seines Klosters Aniane und zur sogenannten "anianischen Reform". Mit kommentierten Editionen der Vita Benedicti Anianensis, Notitia de servitio monasteriorum, des Chronicon Moissacense/Anianense sowie zweier Lokaltraditionen aus Aniane. Thèse de doctorat, soutenue à l'université de Duisbourg, le 19 janvier 2000, dir. Dieter Geuenich', *Revue Mabillon* N. S. 11 (2000) 321–323. This study will, one hopes, elucidate and resolve the problems and open questions regarding this text and its history.
69. See Bonnerue, 'Introduction', 33–35.

described until after Chapter Thirty. The description of new buildings in Chapter Twenty-two is much too sketchy, compared with the description of earlier building projects in Chapter Seventeen, as are accounts of the reform of monasteries in Chapter Twenty-four, when compared with the detailed and more precise accounts in Chapters Thirty-one, Thirty-three, and Thirty-four. Bonnerue wonders why miracle stories are recounted in Chapters Twenty-five to Twenty-eight, when these had already been covered in Chapters Seven to Sixteen. Finally, Benedict's contributions to monastic reform are emphasized in Chapter Twenty-nine. The interpolated section concludes with Benedict's attendance at Aachen, this time, however, under Emperor Louis the Pious, not his father Charlemagne.

This question cannot be resolved without further thorough study, still to be undertaken. We are unwilling to let the problem of conceivable interpolation rest, however. Even if Bonnerue's assumption—that a complete section of no less than eleven and a half chapters is a subsequent addition—should remain unsubstantiated, we must nevertheless stress that other scholars have for some time raised similar charges of interpolation against these chapters.

The controversial assessment of Chapter Thirty is especially crucial. Allen Cabaniss regarded it as a complete interpolation by a later redactor. In this point he apparently concurs with Pierre Tisset's view.[70] Wilhelm Pückert's position is somewhat more cautious. He was able to recognize Ardo of Aniane's style in Chapter Thirty, and considered as later interpolations only certain phrases, those that all too blatantly imply Aniane's dominance over Gellone.[71]

A decree does exist, however, in which William transfers estates to the *cella* Gellone and explicitly places his foundation under Benedict's spiritual and administrative authority, and thereby the authority of the abbey of Aniane. Different versions of this text are extant, preserved in Gellone and Ariane respectively. In the course of their dispute, each house manipulated the charter's text to its own advantage.[72] Yet another version of this charter only recently came into the possession of the

70. Tisset, *L'Abbaye de Gellone*, 8–10 und 55.

71. Pückert, *Aniane und Gellone*, 107–110.

72. For a summary see Chastang, 'Mémoire', 179–182. See also Lemaître and Le Blévec, *Le livre du chapitre*, 36–39, who voice strong doubts regarding the authenticity of the donation charter.

Montpellier archives, and was initially considered to be another eleventh-century Aniane forgery. According to the most recent appraisal, however, it is indeed possible that this document is the original charter issued by William on 15 December 804.[73] Accepting these findings would necessitate abandoning most of the allegations made against Chapter Thirty of the *Life*. The reference to Gellone as a *cella*—a small monastery with only a slight degree of autonomy and dependent on a mother house—would no longer appear offensive if the very founder himself made use of the term. Furthermore, this term is used for Gellone in several charters issued by Louis the Pious, in which Gellone is placed under Aniane's authority. These documents, however, originate from Aniane's cartulary and must therefore be considered probable forgeries. These questions can only be conclusively resolved when the critical edition of Louis the Pious' charters becomes available.[74] The question of whether or not Chapter Thirty of the *Life* has been subjected to interpolation, and if so to what degree, cannot be settled at this juncture. The testimony of the written sources, however, does seem to speak in favor of the view that Ardo could have written this chapter in its present form in the 820's.

Finally, let us cast a brief glance at the beginning section of the passage identified by Bonnerue as a potential interpolation. In 18.3-6 we

73. Archives départementales de l'Hérault, Montpellier, 1 J 1015. For a brief account of how the charter came into the archives' possession see Mersiowsky, 'Zur Edition', 333; re the question of its authenticity see Pierre Chastang, *Lire, écrire, transcrire: le travail des rédacteurs de cartulaires en Bas-Languedoc (XIe–XIIIe siècles)* (Paris: Edition du CTHS, 2001) 154 with note 558. For a summary of its contents, see Chastang, 'Mémoire', 179–182, including an excerpt from the charter's text.

74. Until such an edition is published, the *Regesta Imperii* must be consulted: *Regesta Imperii I: Die Regesten des Kaiserreiches unter den Karolingern 751–918*, nach Johann Friedrich Böhmer neu bearbeitet von Engelbert Mühlbacher (Innsbruck: Verlag der Wagner'schen Universitätsbuchhandlung, ²1908). Individual charters are cited with the abbreviation BM² followed by the entry number. On the work-in-progress on a critical edition, see Theo Kölzer, *Kaiser Ludwig der Fromme (814–840) im Spiegel seiner Urkunden* (Paderborn: Schöningh, 2005). The charters refering to Gellone as *cella* are: BM² 522, 752 und 970. According to a chart in Kölzer's preliminary report, the authenticity of the latter two charters does not appear to be in doubt.

find the text of a charter issued by Charlemagne in 792,[75] which is extant in another version. The second, longer, version containing additional formulaic elements immediately follows the text of the *Vita* in the Aniane cartulary. The charter grants the abbey of Aniane full immunity and the protection of the ruling dynasty. Furthermore, the abbey is granted the right to elect its own abbots. The coupling of these elements is, of course, not common until the charters of Louis the Pious, Charlemagne's son.[76] A confirmation charter of these privileges, issued by Louis, is also preserved.[77] Presumably, the abovementioned charter issued by Charlemagne originally granted only immunity, but not royal protection and the free elections of abbots. In all probability, the content of the version of the charter as it appears in the *Life* is actually a combination of the original charter issued by Charlemagne and the confirmation charter issued by Louis.[78] Inevitably this brings to mind the question whether Ardo was responsible for this fusion or whether this was done in the course of a later redaction of the *Life*. The latter appears the more probable, as the introduction preceding the charter in the text of the *Life* mentions only immunity (18.2). Thus in the original context the reference pertained to Charlemagne's charter in its original form. Whether or not this charter appeared *verbatim* in the *Life*, or whether Ardo's original merely made brief reference to the charter's existence, cannot be resolved here.

Not only the middle section of the *Life*, but also its conclusion has been subject to repeated discussion. Following the text of the *Life* in the Aniane cartulary we find, first, a letter from the monks of Inden (Cornelimünster), in which they give a brief summary of Benedict's career and a more extensive, detailed description of his final days and death. They conclude with a request that Ardo write Benedict's biography and send it to them (Chapter Forty-two). Ardo mentions the letter from the monks of Inden in the *Praefatio* (Preface:b). He explicitly mentions the description of Benedict's death and the request for a *Life*, but ignores the monks' summary of Benedict's life. It is quite possible that Ardo used

75. *Die Urkunden Pippins, Karlmanns und Karls des Großen*, ed. Engelbert Mühlbacher (Hannover: Hahn, 1906) 231–233 (charter no. 173).

76. On the new type of combined privilege, see Kölzer, *Kaiser Ludwig der Fromme*, 27.

77. BM² 524 dated 24 April 814.

78. See Chastang, *Lire*, 162–168.

this summary as the foundation for his more extensive narrative. Adding the letter from the monks of Inden to the text of the *Life*, Ardo picks up on his *Praefatio* and in so doing bestows upon the hagiographical work its actual conclusion. Two more letters follow the one from Inden, letters from Benedict's own pen. In the first (Chapter Forty-three), he takes leave of George, his successor as abbot of Aniane; in the second he takes leave of his old companion Nibridius, Archbishop of Narbonne.

Whether these letters belong to Benedict's *Life*, that appears to come to its natural conclusion with the letter from the monks of Inden, is unclear. It does not automatically follow, however, that these two letters are supplements. It is not impossible that the monks sent these two final documents together with their account of Benedict's death. Naturally they would have retained copies of the letters to George and Nibridius. Why should they not have added them to the account for Ardo? On the other hand, one of the letters is specifically addressed to the abbot and monks of Aniane, so it must have been available there. Ardo undoubtedly had access to it, as he reveals elsewhere in the *Life* that he had access to the charters stored in the monastery's archives. The letter to Nibridius requests the bishop to bestow upon Aniane his special solicitude. It is conceivable that Nibridius provided the abbey with a copy of this letter at some appropriate opportunity. Be that as it may, in both cases it is far from absurd to assume that these two letters somehow came into Ardo's possession. And if this was the case, it is conceivable that he himself appended them to his *Life*. In quality, there is no great difference between the account of the monks of Inden and the two letters by Benedict. In either case, Ardo definitely did not write this material. If Ardo himself added the monks' account to his *Life*, why should he not have done the same with the other letters?

CONCLUSIONS

What conclusion may be drawn from all these confusing, and in part contradictory, considerations? Regardless of the final outcome in the debates over the extent of interpolation and manipulations of the *Life*, we must, in reading it, keep in mind that the text in the middle section was most likely at some time significantly altered, and that in its present form it does not necessarily represent the intentions of Ardo's original testimony.

We must, at the same time, not ignore the fact that major portions of the *Life* may still be regarded as being above suspicion, and that it retains its value as an historical source: Benedict's early career, his close relationship to the Carolingian dynasty—Louis the Pious in particular— as well as his distinguished position in Aquitaine and the empire remain largely untainted by charges of forgery. Unaffected also are the descriptions of his character, his piety, and his political activities, as well as the details regarding his literary pursuits. Nor do the colorful descriptions of daily life in an early medieval monastery lose any of their charm or value.

ARDO OF ANIANE

Our final task is to cast a brief glance at Ardo of Aniane himself (783-843), the author of the *Life*. In high medieval written sources from Aniane, Ardo is honored with a nickname: *Ardo, qui est Smaragdus*.[79] Because of this 'title', he came to be confused with another monastic author, Smaragdus, abbot of Saint-Mihiel. In his study on the abbot of Saint-Mihiel, who was active in the monastic reform movement by means of his *Commentary* on the Rule of Benedict[80] and a treatise for monks on monastic virtues (*Diadema monachorum*), and was also well known through his theological writings, Fidel Rädle devotes a detailed segment to Ardo of Aniane. The likeness in name caused confusion well into the twentieth century, and in discussions of individual works by Smaragdus, repeated attempts were made to attribute them to the monk of Aniane. Rädle's studies should have resolved these questions once and for all. Ardo was held in high esteem within the local tradition of Aniane, even after his death. They were proud of him as a master teacher. There is no mention anywhere, however, of his literary pursuits. Three extant epitaphs corroborate this: one (a fragment) is found on a tomb-

---

79. Fidel Rädle, *Studien zu Smaragd von Saint-Mihiel* (München: Fink, 1974) 79–96.

80. *Smaragdi Abbatis Expositio in Regulam S. Benedicti*, edd. Alfredus Spannagel and Pius Engelbert OSB, in Kassius Hallinger OSB, general editor, Corpus Consuetudinum Monasticarum, 8 (Siegburg:Verlag Franz Schmitt, 1974). English translation by David Barry OSB, *Smaragdus of Saint-Mihiel, Commentary on the Rule of Saint Benedict*, Cistercian Studies series, 212 (Kalamazoo: Cistercian Publications, 2008).

stone in Aniane; the other two texts are preserved in manuscripts.[81]
Rädle's conclusion is clear: none of the works by Smaragdus of Saint-
Mihiel can be accredited to Ardo.

How did this confusion of identities arise?[82] One can only speculate.
It appears, however, that the nickname 'Smaragdus' is primarily used in
the so-called *Chronicon Arianense,*[83] an historiographically unreliable text
dating from the eleventh or twelfth century. Within this text Smaragdus
appears exclusively in the context of descriptions of events that are
definitely fictitious. Since the famous Smaragdus of Saint-Mihiel was
actually in contact with Benedict of Aniane and the reformers of monasticism, it is therefore quite conceivable that Aniane attempted to
magnify its own significance by adorning itself with this name. There
might be a possible link to the dispute with Gellone in this context.
The close bond of the Aniane tradition to Smaragdus would also explain
the appearance of verses written by Smaragdus of Saint-Mihiel in the
space between the two letters appended to the *Life.*[84]

Rädle also analyzes the *Life's* linguistic properties,[85] disclosing numerous violations of Latin grammar and characterizing Ardo's Latin as
'flawed' and 'extremely labored'.[86] Ardo's transgressions include the use
of original and unusual word-forms, errors in gender, incorrect syntax,
and—one of the most conspicuous idiosyncrasies—the frequent use of
the accusative absolute. More recent studies, in particular those of Bengt
Löfstedt, have contributed further examples which complement Rädle's
observations.[87] Thomas Haye partially exonerates Ardo by drawing attention to the fact that the phenomena described were not all that
unusual in Ardo's day and therefore not subject to generalizations as

81. Printed in: MGH Poetae 4 1031 (no. 10 and 11) and MGH Poetae 6 141
(no. 6), also in: Rädle, *Studien,* 80–82.
82. See Rädle, *Studien,* 86–96.
83. Printed together with the *Chronicon Moissiacense,* ed. Pertz, 280–313. The
nicknames occur on 301, lines 27 and 30, 310, line 49, and 311 line 31, though the
last reference is not to Ardo, but to an abbot of Aniane named Smaragdus.
84. Rädle, *Studien,* 89 f.
85. Rädle, *Studien,* 84–86.
86. Rädle, *Studien,* 84. This view concurs with opinions voiced by Georg Waitz,
MGH SS 15,1 199.
87. Bengt Löfstedt, 'Zu Ardos "Vita s. Benedicti"', *Aevum* 59 (1985) 178–180.

being violations of grammar.[88] Providing numerous examples, Haye demonstrates that Ardo varies his language according to his subject matter: the narrative passages are written in a simple, clear style, whereas the reflective portions tend to be rhetorically more elaborate.[89] Ardo's vocabulary tends to be plain, marked by the repetitious use of specific words and phrases.[90] Moreover, a certain propinquity to the style of legal documents of the period is perceptible—an observation that might indirectly underscore Ardo's credibility and make it all the more plausible that he referred to charters when composing the *Life*.[91]

When evaluating the linguistic quality of Ardo's text, we must also take into consideration its late transmission. Minor alterations like word-endings, prefixes, and various sentence structures may just as likely have been the product of a later transcription. When evidence for the quality of Ardo's style of Latin is taken from the very chapters that are under acute suspicion of being interpolated—as much as one fifth to one quarter of the entire text[92]—the question becomes especially problematic.

For valuable suggestions we wish to thank Professor Dr Mark Mersiowsky and Professor Dr Gerhard Schmitz of the Monumenta Germaniae Historica.

Annette Grabowsky and Clemens Radl

Universität Tübingen and Monumenta Germaniae Historica
English translation by Cornelia Oefelein

---

88. Thomas Haye, '*Solecismorum fetor*: Einige philologische Bemerkungen zu Ardo von Aniane', *Archivum Latinitatis Medii Aevi* 52 (1994) 151–166.

89. Haye, '*Solecismorum fetor*', 163f.

90. For example Ardo's frequent use of the word *pandere*, the stereotype use of *vice alia* when listing Benedict's deeds and his fondness for compounding adjectives with the prefixes *pre-* and *per-*; see Haye, '*Solecismorum fetor*', 164f.

91. Haye, '*Solecismorum fetor*', 165f.

92. Georg Waitz, MGH SS 1 199, remarked on the interdependency between the datings of the transcription and the cartulary; see also the brief remarks by L.-H. Lucassen, 'À propos d'un texte de la vie de s. Benoît d'Aniane par Ardon', *Archivum Latinitatis Medii Aevi* 4 (1928) 78 f.

TRANSLATOR'S INTRODUCTION

THE LIFE OF BENEDICT

From the *Vita Benedicti* by Ardo, here translated, and the letters appended to it, the following chronological data concerning Benedict of Aniane can be extracted. His death date is precisely given as 11 February 821, a Monday (42.5).[1] The same note states that he was in his seventies (*septuagenarius*) when he died. His birth was therefore about 750 AD. A day or two before his demise he told his followers that he had been a monk for forty-eight years (42.4). Thus the year of his profession was about 773. Three years earlier than that, about 770, he was inflamed with a desire to abandon secular activity and he had undertaken ascetic practices (1.2). But he delayed making a formal decision until 'the year that Italy was made subject to the sway of glorious King Charles', the great Charlemagne (2.1). That Italian (more properly, Lombard) war was fought, as we know from other sources, in 773–774.[2] Hence the previous dating is approximately accurate.

Before his first feeling of a call to the religious life, Benedict was reared at the court of King Pepin (reigned, 751–768), Charles's father, where he ultimately became a cupbearer (*princerna*). When he was old enough he entered the military service of Pepin until the latter's death (768). After that and upon Charles's accession—first as joint king with his brother, Carloman, then in 771 as sole king—he continued in the

---

1. The day, month, and year are given in the text as indicated. The day of the week was determined by use of Erich Bornmann, *Zeitrechnung und Kirchenjahr* and *Calendarium perpetuum* (Kassel: J. Stauda, 1964). Watkin Williams, 'St Benedict of Aniane', *Downside Review* 54 (July 1936) 374, says it was a Friday.

2. For sources, see Allen Cabaniss, *Charlemagne* (New York: Twayne, 1972) 18f.

royal army (1.1).The age of fifteen or thereabout was a usual period at which one was girded with the sword.[3] For about five years, then, Benedict was a soldier, as his father had been before him (1.1).

The place of Benedict's profession as monk was the abbey of Saint Seine near Dijon (2.2).There he remained for two and a half years, according to Ardo and the letter mentioned above (2.3; 42.1). But Ardo contradicted himself, for in another passage (3.1) he intimated the duration was five years and eight months.The discrepancy has been quite reasonably resolved by assuming the two and a half years to refer to Benedict's monastic experience before he was appointed cellarer and the five and two thirds years to the whole time elapsed since his profession.[4] Benedict therefore left Saint Seine about 779.

Another fairly definite date in the *Vita* emerges by allusion to a 'very severe' (*gravissima*) famine (7.1).That could be the one (*vero magna*) mentioned in the annals of Lorsch for 779.[5] But it was more likely the (*validissima*) famine of 793 recorded in the chronicle of Moissac,[6] because of the statement, 'at the same time the baneful doctrine of Felicianism' invaded the Midi (8.1).That is known to have occurred during the interval 789-792.[7] Felix abjured his erroneous teaching in 792, but in 793 relapsed into it, eluded his jailers, and fled to Muslim Spain.[8] The *Vita* is in consequence probably correct in stating that the famine and the heresy occurred 'at the same time' (7.1; 8.1).

Three other dates are given: one explicitly; the others by inference. The first was 782, the year in which Benedict undertook an expansive building program for Aniane (17.2).This was particularly important

3. The anonymous life of Louis, I, 6.1, translated in Allen Cabaniss, *Son of Charlemagne* (Syracuse: Syracuse University Press, 1961) 37; Allen Cabaniss, *Judith Augusta: A Daughter-in-Law of Charlemagne, and Other Essays* (New York: Vantage Press, 1974) 18.

4. Williams, 'St Benedict of Aniane', 359f. See Sigurd Abel, *Jahrbücher des fränkischen Reichs unter Karl dem Grossen,* 1 (2nd edition with Bernhard von Simson (Leipzig: Duncker und Humblot, 1888) 439f.

5. SS 1:31.

6. *Chronicon Moissiacense;* SS 1:300.

7. See Allen Cabaniss, 'Felix of Urgel, Archheretic', in Cabaniss, *Judith Augusta,* 67; originally published as 'The Heresiarch Felix', *Catholic Historical Review* 39:2 (July 1953) 129–141.

8. *Judith Augusta,* 69.

because he changed his style completely; whereas he had in the past allowed only the crudest structures (5.2), he now unaccountably permitted elaborate and rich ornamentation (17.2). The second date, ten years later, is implied. Embedded in the *Vita* (18.3-6) is a text of 'immunity' granted by Charles to Benedict and Aniane.[9] Another royal charter, dated June 799,[10] confirming to Benedict the estate of Celleneuve is also suggested, but there is no certainty about it (19.1). The third date, 816–818, is indicated by reference to a great assembly at Aix-la-Chapelle,[11] an effort to bring some degree of uniformity to monastic practice in the carolingian domain, an action that seemed to be an imperial attempt to set Benedict 'over all the monasteries' in the realm (36.1).

In addition to chronological data, the *Vita* offers the following information about its protagonist. He was born in Gothia 'of the nation of the Getae' and 'of noble origin'. His father (unnamed) was a count of Maguelonne,[12] a loyal adherent of the Frankish government and an effective military chieftain, noted especially for his crushing defeat of marauding Basques. He entrusted his young son to King Pepin's court. There Benedict was one of the 'queen's [Bertrada's] scholars', beloved by his peers in age, nimble-witted, and adaptable. Rising to prominence in such surroundings, he entered those military duties expected of a youth of his status (1.1).

At about the age of twenty Benedict was for some reason attracted to religious life. Although he continued to perform his obligations at court, he brooded over the strong appeal of religion and began to practice austerities (1.2). Uncertain of the effect an open decision might have on his father, he hesitated about the particular future expression of his desire. Among the possibilities were becoming a lifelong pilgrim,

9. See J. Böhmer, E. Mühlbacher, J. Lechner, *Die Regesten des Kaiserreichs unter den Karolingern 751–918* (Innsbruck: Verlag der Wagner'schen Universitäts-Buchhandlung, 1908). No. 318. Hereinafter cited as Mühlbacher, *Regesta*.

10. *Ibid.*, No. 340.

11. There were three gatherings at Aix-la-Chapelle: August 816, July 817, and July 818. See David Knowles, *From Pachomius to Ignatius* (Oxford: Clarendon Press, 1966) 8. But compare Josef Semmler, 'Die Beschluß des Aachener Konzils im Jahr 816', *Zeitschrift für Kirchengeschichte*, 74 (1963).

12. His name is given as Aigulf by Herbert Thurston and Donald Attwater, *Butler's Lives of the Saints*, 1 (New York: P. J. Kenedy and Sons, 1956) 309.

becoming a shepherd or herdsman in the countryside without pay, or becoming a shoemaker[13] in some city and sustaining his work among the poor by the labor of his hands (1.3).

The event that forced him to a decision was an encounter with death. He witnessed his brother trying recklessly to ford a raging river, presumably in north Italy. Riding into the flood in an attempt—whether successful, we are not informed—to rescue his brother, Benedict himself was almost drowned. In the narrow escape Benedict, like Martin Luther over seven centuries later, vowed to abandon the world. At once he returned to his homeland (2.1). Still hesitant to discuss his problem with his father, he confided in a blind solitary named Widmar, who was able to advise him, yet maintain the secret. In an act of deception comparable to that of Bodo-Eleazar more than fifty years later,[14] Benedict made ostensible plans to go to Aix-la-Chapelle and appear before King Charles. But when he and his companions reached the community of Sainte Seine, he suddenly threw off the cloak of secrecy, dismissed his escort, and in due course made profession as monk (2.2).

During his time at Saint Seine—perhaps five and two thirds years (3.1), less likely two and a half (2.3)—Benedict practiced excessive fasting, weeping, sleeplessness, and prayer (2.3-5). He performed menial tasks for his brothers, wore the meanest garments, avoided bathing, and allowed his body to be covered by lice which gnawed as his flesh (2.4). The abbot tried to persuade, even to compel, him to moderate his rigor, but Benedict churlishly declared that the famous *Rule* of the man whose name he bore was fit only for novices and weaklings who were capable merely of doing things within the realm of possibility (2.5). He himself preferred, so he said, the harsher precepts of Basil[15] and Pachomius[16], who advocated striving to achieve impossible things. Not content to

13. The Latin word is *sutor*, which Williams, 'St Benedict of Aniane', 358, renders as *taklor*.

14. Allen Cabaniss, 'Bodo-Eleazar, Convert to Judaism', in *Judith Augusta*, 106–122; originally published as 'Bodo-Eleazar: A Famous Jewish Convert', *Jewish Quarterly Review* 43:4 (April 1953) 318–328.

15. *c.* 329–379, metropolitan of Cappadocian Caesarea, exegete, theologian, and author of ascetical works which form the basis of Eastern Christian monasticism.

16. 292–346, the founder of Egyptian monastic communities and author of the first known cenobitical works. See Armand Veilleux, trans. *Pachomian Koinonia*, 3 volumes (Kalamazoo: Cistercian Publications, 1980–1982).

practice austerities in private, he took it upon himself publicly to challenge the manners of his fellows, to scold, exhort, admonish, and upbraid (2.3-5).

For a while he served the community as cellarer. That office afforded him an opportunity to commit the Benedictine *Rule* to memory, a feat which probably led him to relax his attachment to the life prescribed by his eastern mentors. All the while he took his duty seriously. In distribution he was generous to those who sought in what he deemed a lawful manner, but refused those who sought 'unlawfully'. For that reason he fell into disfavor with many of the brothers. Yet in providing for guests, children, and poor folk, he exercised gentle care and the abbot was quite fond of him (2.6).

It was apparently during Benedict's 'tour' as cellarer that the abbot died. Despite his style of life, there was a perverse demand by the brothers for him to become abbot. But when he assessed the position, he realized, wisely, that sharp internal strife would result. In his awareness Benedict was more discreet than Peter Abelard as abbot of Saint Gildas was at a later time.[17] As hurriedly as he had gone to and entered Saint Seine, he now deserted it and returned to his father's estates. There, on the banks of a stream called Aniane, near the Saône river, he, about thirty years of age, and a few like-minded companions (including Widmar, the blind solitary) erected a hut so they could dwell near a small church of Saint Saturninus (3.1). He and his community lived, worked, and prayed there in deepest poverty. Kindly women of the neighborhood occasionally brought them milk and nearby clergy gave them encouragement (3.1-3; 4.2). Benedict is said to have baked bread for his followers and to have hauled wood on his own shoulders to construction sites, but also to have found opportunity to write a book (5.1), to preach to and instruct the brothers (4.1), and to say Mass (5.1, 3; 21.1). When and where he received Holy Orders is not indicated in the *Vita*, but in the mid-820s Ermoldus Nigellus referred to the then late Benedict as *sacerdos* (priest).[18]

With the passage of time the community grew, so that more and more buildings were required. Benedict insisted on the cheapest timber, thatched roofs, and no ornamentation (5.2). But as Aniane's reputation

17. See *The Story of Abelard's Adversities*, translated J. T. Muckle (Toronto: Pontifical Institute of Mediæval Studies, 1964) 41.

18. Ermoldus Nigellus, *In honorem Hludowici*, II, line 555; PLAC, 2:40.

for holiness and good works spread (5.1), with fame came also fortune.
People began to bestow land and wealth upon the foundation (5.3; 6;
17.2), and, as we noted earlier, a subtle change took place in Benedict.
About his thirty-second or thirty-third year he began to sponsor sump-
tuous buildings (17.2). One monastic church is described glowingly by
Ardo (17.3) in terms that anticipate Abbot Suger's boasts about the
treasures of Saint Denis.[19] It was covered with red tiles, not thatch; it
had painted paneling and marble columns to sustain the cloister porches
(5.2; 17.2). Multiple altars, lamps, and candelabra, intricately contrived,
are mentioned (17.3-6). An important library was assembled as were
costly vestments and silver vessels. It became a school for cantors and
lectors, for grammarians and Scripture scholars.[20] Indeed several of
Benedict's students were elevated to the episcopate (18.1).

Looking back over his life thus far we may logically discern three
'conversions' that Benedict underwent. The first, his 'evangelical' experience, was an emotional shift from secular to religious interests about
770 (1.2); the second, his monastic profession about 774 (2.2); and the
third, his relaxation of rigors about 782 (17.2; 21.1). His biographer
considered the last a decline (*declinarat*, 21.1), but we may perhaps deem
it an intellectual change.

Benedict's several 'conversions' were reflected in his attitude toward
the famous benedictine *Rule*. At his first conversion, while still wonder-
ing what to do with his life, he fell in love with it, but at Sainte Seine
he tended to denigrate it by comparison with more severe eastern rules.
Yet he was unable to abandon his attachment to it and during his time
as cellarer he memorized it (2.6). When he became the superior of an
ever increasing number of monasteries, he devoted himself to intensive
study and mastery of the *Rule*, visiting various communities to inquire
of experts what he did not know or understand. For the sake of comparison, he assembled a library of as many different rules as he could
discover (18.1). In his visits Benedict made a practice of explaining
obscurities in it (20) and as a result his followers were steeped in its
teaching and discipline.

19. See Erwin Panofsky, *Abbot Suger on the Abbey Church of St.-Denis and its Art
Treasures* (Princeton: Princeton University Press, 1946) *passim*, especially 63.

20. The Latin is *scientia scripturarum peritos*, not simply 'those expert in written compositions'—*pace* Arthur J. Zuckerman, *A Jewish Princedom in Feudal France
768–900* (New York: Columbia University Press, 1972) 212.

At King Louis's insistence, Benedict traveled throughout Aquitaine reviving the *Rule* where it had fallen into desuetude (18.1; 29.1). So often did he visit many monasteries to discuss it chapter by chapter that it is no wonder numerous counts accused him of being 'a wandering monk' (29.3). After Louis the Pious' accession to the empire, Benedict was responsible for revival of the *Rule* in Frankland (35; 36.1). He played a leading role at the council of Aachen / Aix-la-Chapelle (816–818) by his expositions (36.1). The *Rule*, it was said, was his greatest study. He made a practice of interrogating scholars both near at hand and at a distance (18.1; 38.6). Visitors on their way to Monte Cassino were asked to note both what they heard and what they saw, and then to report to him (38.6). Finally he compiled a book, *Concordia regularum* (A Harmony of the Rules), quoting passages from other rules to show the superiority of Saint Benedict's (38.7).

By 792 Aniane was head of a family of monastic communities, not only in Gothia, but also in other parts of the carolingian world (18.1). Ten years earlier King Charles had already granted significant 'immunity' to Aniane and its complex (18.3-6); he continued to do so as late as 799 (19.1), by which time he may have been involved in his imperial adventure. As early as 792 or thereabout Benedict, too, was deeply embroiled in extra-monastic activity. He and others were, for instance, busily engaged in campaigning in southern Gaul and perhaps Spain against Felix of Urgel[21] and his teaching (8.1). Because of his varied labors and the reputation of his monks for sanctity, Benedict was well known among all classes. His turn from the rigor of his first way of life, while perhaps disappointing to his biographer, was nonetheless recognized by Ardo as necessary because 'he had undertaken an impossible task'. But Benedict's purpose remained, so he plowed, dug, and reaped along with others (21.1). He maintained his abstinence from meat and wine, except when he was ill; then he took some chicken broth (21.2). He also pursued in an unusual manner his pastoral care, being able to cure others of the typical monastic malaise of *acedia* or melancholy (21.4).

The fame of his monks became so widespread that eminent prelates asked for some of the monks to inaugurate, to strengthen, or to reform their own communities. Among them, Bishop Leidrad of Lyons, Bishop

---

21. Felix, bishop of Urgel in Spain, (d. 818) was held responsible for adoptionist teaching there.

Theodulf of Orléans, and Abbot Alcuin of Saint Martin of Tours sought Benedict's students (24.1, 2, 5). In 814 and the years afterwards, Louis, originally king of Aquitaine, but by then successor of Charlemagne, his father, as 'emperor of the whole church in Europe' (29.1), having already discovered Benedict's way of holiness (19.2; 31.1; 33.34), 'set him over all the monasteries in the realm' (29.1). Good Queen Irmingard, too, admired him (31.1). As a result Benedict was summoned to Marmoutier in Alsace. Even that place was not close enough to Louis, so the emperor removed him to a small new monastic settlement on the river Inde very near Aix-la-Chapelle. Thus Benedict could always be available for consultation at the palace (35.1, 2).

Despite Benedict's powerful friends, the *Vita* did not neglect his enemies. The earliest were his fellows at Saint Seine, whom he irritated with his exceptional austerities (2.4). Others were some of his own students at Aniane (3.2; 10, 16).[22] Still others were sneering layfolk who despised his movement (26, 29.3). As Benedict advanced in public esteem, some of the secular clergy tried to minimize his activities. Some of the nobility, envious of his position, condemned him as a vagabond, greedy for property (29.3). But before his death his friends outnumbered his enemies in influence and importance.

It is worthy of note that the *Vita* does not gloss over certain aspects of its hero's life that were not admirable. To us moderns perhaps the most unfavorable feature was Benedict's physical filthiness: the few baths he took during his lifetime, the lice crawling over his body, and his refusal to change clothes more frequently than at forty-day intervals (2.4; 43.2). Even Ardo remarked that his threadbare, patched cowls 'rendered him somewhat unsightly' (2.4). His extreme 'finickiness' in eating must have been a trial to those in the kitchen of his monastery (21.2, 3) and his habit of scolding did not endear him (2.5). His sharp disagreement with his abbot at Saint Seine did not set a good example (2.5); in fact the word to describe it is *churlish*. Ecstatics he looked upon as rude (9), a strange description coming from Benedict. Even in his own day his manner of life was deemed new and strange (3.2), and Benedict's disgust with those who did not persevere in it was not encouraging.

When time came for a change, the reason for it was left unexplained in the *Vita*. Some of it was attributed to his realization of impossibilities

---

22. See his letter to his student Guarnarius, EppKA 2:561-563.

involved in his earlier way (17.2, 21.1). Some of it was indeed compromise for the sake not only of human frailty, but also for the sake of appearance (37.2)—a curious characterization of the austere Benedict, but perhaps experience was having a didactic effect. It is perhaps significant that his religious life had begun in deception (2.1, 2), for apparently he misled his father and many of his companions when he experienced a monastic conversion.

From the first years of Louis's reign as emperor Benedict's constant attendance on him caused his biographer to state that he wore 'away the palace floors'. All who suffered injuries from others or who sought imperial opinions used him as intermediary (35.3). Many laymen besieged him with questions 'about direction of the realm, about disposition of provinces, and about their own advantage'. But Benedict, although desirous of assisting everyone, gave his primary attention to the needs of monks (35.4). By that time he had become a devoted advocate of the moderate *Rule* of Saint Benedict (37.2). Even as he interpreted it, however, he showed willingness to make concessions and compromises (36.1; 37, 38), and indeed to contrive devotional practices not mentioned in the *Rule* (38).[23] He made special effort, at least partially successful, to free monasteries and their communities from lay usurpation and sequestration (39).

During his last five years (42.5) Benedict's vigils, tears, fasting, reading, and meditation (41.1), together with the lack of cleanliness (41.2), took their toll on his life as surely as the physical exertion and the oversight of twelve communities (42.2),[24] and he began to waste away. His final illness started on 7 and 8 February 821 (42.3; 43.4). On 9 February he was removed from his room at Aix to his monastery of Inde (42.4), where on 11 February, the first Monday of Lent, he died, surrounded by his followers. Two days later (that is, 'on the third day') he was buried there in a stone sepulcher ordered by Emperor Louis (42.5).

23. Edmund Bishop, 'On the Origin of the Prymer', in his *Liturgica Historica* (Oxford: Clarendon Press, 1918) 211–237, especially 211–214, 236f.

24. Twelve foundations are listed in Ardo's *Vita Benedicti* as indicated, but Josef Semmler, 'Karl der Grosse und das Fränkische Mönchtum', in Wolfgang Braunfels, ed., *Karl der Grosse: Lebenswerk und Nachleben* (Düsseldorf: L. Schwann, 1965) 2: 255–289, especially 260, adds a possible thirteenth and suggests that thirty-eight others were strongly influenced by Benedict.

The Works of Benedict

In the *Vita* there are numerous references to writings by Benedict, few of which have survived. The first was an unidentified work done early in his career while cooking in the kitchen (5.1). The second was a collection of all the rules he could discover (this may allude to the gathering of a library, 18.1). The third was Benedict's compilation of a decree for the emperor's seal, summarizing action of the council of Aachen that strove to bring monastic uniformity in Frankland (38.6). The fourth was a letter to Louis concerning the *Rule* (*ibid.*). The fifth was a compilation (under Benedict's direction) from the rules of various Fathers to be read at the morning assembly (38.7). The sixth was another book called *Concordia regularum* (*ibid.*). The seventh was still another compilation from the 'sermons of holy teachers' intended to be read at the evening assemblies (*ibid.*). Finally there was a record, found after his death, of 'every office he had performed during the five years and two months' preceding his decease (42.5). It is an amazing list, suggesting the important intellectual interest and equipment of the man.

Additional Sources

The foregoing paragraphs constitute the life of Benedict as derived from Ardo's account. For further data one must have recourse to sources apart from the *Vita*, but they are sparse, only 'some small islands . . . that emerge here and there in an ocean of forgetfulness and silence.'[25] We find, however, that his name before profession was Vitiza (or Witiza), and must have been employed occasionally after his monastic profession, for it was given in the chronicle of Moissac at the year 794, recording his presence in Frankfurt at the council which debated the issues of Felicianism and images. The statement is *Benedictus qui vocatur Vitiza* (Benedict who is called Vitiza—note the present tense of the verb).[26] Vitiza may be the name latinized to *Euticius* in the *Vita* (1.23) of Saint Odo, second abbot of Cluny (*c.* 879–942), as the person for whom Emperor Louis erected a monastery near the palace,[27] unless *Euticius*

---

25. The quotation is from Pierre Tisset, *L'Abbaye de Gellone au diocèse de Lodève des origines au XIIIᵉ siècle* (Paris: Recueil Sirey, 1933) 3.
26. SS 1:301.
27. PL 133:53D-54A.

(*Eutychius*) is a hellenized version of *Benedictus* (both words mean *fortunate*). He may even have been named for one of the last Visigothic kings of Spain: Witiza, 700–710.[28] Additional facts are derived from the correspondence of Alcuin (*c.* 735–804), abbot of Saint Martin at Tours.[29] He and Benedict were friends before Alcuin went to Tours in 796. Not only did Benedict offer prayers for Alcuin, but he also sent him some medicinal herbs for which the latter dispatched a note of thanks.[30] Alcuin also submitted some of his letters for Benedict's comments and for delivery to the appropriate persons, one indeed to King Charles.[31] After Alcuin became abbot of Saint Martin's, he founded a new congregation about eight miles away at Cormery (as we learn from Ardo's *Vita*, 24.5), the first contingent of monks being some he had requested from Benedict's care—this we learn in a letter to his friend, Bishop Arno of Salzburg.[32] In 800 he wrote to Leidrad, bishop of Lyons (799–815), Nibridius, abbot of La Grasse, then bishop of Narbonne (*c.* 799–*c.* 822), and Benedict concerning a new journey they were undertaking, on Charles's order, to preach against the Felician heresy in the area between the Loire and Ebro rivers.[33] From it we learn that it was the second such trip the three had made. Shortly thereafter Alcuin wrote another letter to the same three on the same subject.[34] After that came a letter to all the monastic establishments of Gothia. In it he discussed a book which he had written against the heresy and which he had transmitted to them by Abbot Benedict.[35] Then he sent a letter to Nibridius commending Benedict, with whom he had just talked and who was then on his way to Nibridius.[36] Almost immediately a letter went to his friend Arno. It told of Felix's imprisonment at Lyons and of the three clerics' visit *in illas*

28. See Barnard S. Bachrach, 'A Reassessment of Visigothic Jewish Policy', *American Historical Review* 78:1 (February 1973) 11–34.

29. See Eleanor S. Duckett, *Alcuin, Friend of Charlemagne: His World and His Work* (New York: Macmillan Co., 1951); Max Manitius, *Geschichte der lateinischen Literatur des Mittelalters,* 1 (Munich: Beck, 1911) 273–288.

30. Alcuin, *Epistola* 56; EppKA 2:99f.

31. *Epistola* 57; EppKA 2:100f.

32. *Epistola* 184; EppKA 2:309f.

33. *Epistola* 200; EppKA 2:330-333.

34. *Epistola* 201: EppKA 2:333f.

35. *Epistola* 205; EppKA 2:340-342.

36. *Epistola* 206; EppKA 2:342f.

partes occidentales (into those western regions) to extinguish the faithless doctrine.[37]

The author of Alcuin's life related that Benedict visited Alcuin for counsel concerning his own salvation and that of his students in Gothia. Alcuin is supposed to have been able clairvoyantly to anticipate Benedict's approach and to have sent forward an escort to accompany him, but he declined to satisfy Benedict's curiosity about the occurrence. The two men were so intimate that Alcuin revealed to Benedict his own special private prayer and Benedict presumed to suggest an additional petition, to which the former happily replied, 'So be it, most revered son, so be it'.[38] The author advised those who could not follow in the steps of the ancient churchmen to follow those who lived more recently, who were approved by Christ, and who were worthy of imitation, namely, 'for monks Benedict [of Aniane] and for canons Alcuin.'[39]

Theodulf (*c.* 750–821), bishop of Orléans, wrote a poem for Aniane's monks and Benedict.[40] To the latter he declared, 'What Benedict [of Nursia] was as director in Italian lands, so you, Benedict [of Aniane], are in our lands'.[41] He asked for assistance and Benedict dispatched two monks (line 11). So successful were they that Benedict later sent him 'twice ten' (24.2). Theodulf added some other names of Benedict's friends—that is, other than himself: Nibridius; Atilio, abbot of Saint Thibéry; and Anianus, abbot of Saints John and Lawrence, (3.1); Donatus (line 68); Nampius or Nampio (line 71), abbot of Saint Hilary near Carcassonne; Orlemundus (line 72), abbot of Montolieu; Clarinus, Teutfredus, and Leubila (line 77). He mentioned Atilius (line 77; presumably the same as Atilio, 3.1, 3), Atala (line 72), and Attila (line 77)—the latter two also perhaps the same as Atilio, or was Atala the abbot from Spain in whose company Agobard came to Septimania?[42]

37. Epistola 207; EppKA 2:343-345. Alcuin addressed also *Epistola* 303 (*ibid.*, 461f.) to Nibridius and Benedict, exhorting them to assiduity in their labors.

38. *Vita Alcuini*, 19; SS 15, Part 1:184-197.

39. *Ibid., prologus.*

40. Manitius, *Geschichte*, 1:537-543.

41. Theodulf, Carmen XXX, 'Ad monachos sancti Benedicti'; PLAC 1:520-522. The quotation above is from lines 23f. Other lines will be cited internally.

42. Allen Cabaniss, *Agobard of Lyons: Churchman and Critic* (Syracuse University Press, 1953) 4. A more recent book on Agobard is Egon Boshof, *Erzbischof Agobard von Lyon: Leben und Werk* (Vienna: Böhlau Verlag, 1969); on which see my remarks in *Catholic Historical Review* (October 1974) 480f.

To complete the list it may be fitting to note the persons mentioned in Ardo's *Vita* as Benedict's acquaintances in one way or another. By name we have Ardo (d. 843; see 16; 21.2; see also below, The Author and Text), Helisachar, abbot of Saint Riquier and imperial chancellor (i; 42.3; 43.4),[43] King Pepin (1.1), King (Emperor) Charles (1.1; 18.1),[44] blind Widmar (2.2; 3.1), Atilio (3.1, 3), Nibridius (3.1; 44.1), Anianus (3.1), Leidrad (24.1), Theodulf (24.2), Alcuin (24.5), Louis the Pious (29.1; 42.2),[45] Andoar (31.1), Wulfar (a relative of William of Gellone; 34; cf. 30 and below, WILLIAM OF GELLONE), Stabilis, bishop of Maguelonne (41.4); Tanculf, chief of the royal fisc (42.4);[46] Deidonus, Leovigild, Bertrad, Desiderius (42.6), George, third abbot of Aniane (819–822; 43.1), and Modan (43.3). Six persons are mentioned but not by name: Benedict's father (1.1), Queen Bertrada, mother of Charlemagne (d. 783; 1.1), Benedict's brother (2.1), the abbot of Saint Seine (2.6), Felix, the heretical bishop of Urgel (8.1),[47] and the Empress Irmingard (d. 818), first wife of Louis the Pious, or possibly Empress Judith (*c.* 805–844),[48] Louis's second wife (31.4; 42.3).

Benedict's compilations that have survived are a collection of rules (part I, of Eastern Fathers; part II, of Western Fathers; and part III, for nuns)[49] and the *Concordia regularum.*[50] Imperial charters issued in favor of Aniane during Benedict's lifetime were one by Charles and nine by Louis.[51]

Only three letters by Benedict are extant. One, to his student Guarnarius, was written about the time of Felician activity.[52] The student, otherwise unknown, seems to have fallen into that heresy, but the evidence is not conclusive. The note is a miscellany of passages from Scripture along with one from Isidore (*c.* 560–636), bishop of Seville, one from Augustine (354–430), bishop of Hippo, and one from Leo I (pope,

---

43. Bishop, *Liturgica Historica,* (as in note 23), 333–348.
44. See Cabaniss, *Charlemagne* (as in note 2).
45. See Cabaniss, *Son of Charlemagne* (as in note 3).
46. *Ibid.,* 81.
47. See Cabaniss, 'Felix of Urgel' (as in note 7).
48. Benedict probably knew both empresses. On Judith, see Cabaniss, *Judith Augusta* (as in note 3).
49. PL 103:393D-702.
50. *Ibid.,* 703A-1380B.
51. *Ibid.,* 1419B-1431A.
52. EppKA 2:561-563.

440–461), together with an allusion to a formula of faith that Benedict had written. The other two letters, appended to the *Vita*, were written—dictated—on the eve of his death: one, to Abbot George of Aniane, encouraged him to keep up his good work and to consider Abbot Helisachar a trustworthy friend (43); the other, to Bishop Nibridius, asked him to continue his kindly interest in Aniane (44).

Reactions to the life and work of Benedict of Aniane varied, as we have seen, in his lifetime. Within the last century they have been expressed on one hand by Edmund Bishop, 'After the great founder himself, Benedict of Nursia, no man has more widely affected Western monachism than did the second Benedict, he of Aniane';[53] on the other, by David Knowles's comment on that judgment, 'This is put strongly, perhaps too strongly, for the two differed in kind as well as in degree; Benedict of Aniane has never been a spiritual guide for monks'.[54]

THE AUTHOR AND TEXT

After Benedict's death some of his associates at Inde, namely, Deidonus, Leovigild, Bertrad, and Desiderius, addressed a letter to Ardo, teacher and monk of Aniane, request that he compose a *Vita* of Benedict (42). With the letter they sent along some notes they had assembled about their late abbot (42.6). The exact date of that communication is not known. Calling himself 'a slave of Christ's servants'—almost the title *servant of the servants of God* employed by Pope Gregory the Great—Ardo stated that, by the time he began to prepare the *Vita*, it was 'a long time ago' (*iam pridem*) that the letter had been delivered to him. At first Ardo demurred, alleging humility as well as his lack of urbanity, ability, and training. He hoped that someone better qualified would undertake the task. The brothers, however, importuned him. A certain sentimental aura at Aniane, Benedict's original foundation, also affected Ardo (or so he intimated) and impelled him to acquiesce in the request. Still further, Abbot Helisachar was apparently urging him to accept. And there was, despite some timidity, a genuine scholarly impulse to write. Ardo was aware that in the lay world matters and events were recorded for future generations. So in the religious world there was need for the same thing

53. Bishop, *Liturgica Historica*, 213.

54. David Knowles, *The Monastic Order in England* (Cambridge: University Press, 1949) 28, note 2.

lest 'obliging forgetfulness and scurrying time' obliterate important occurrences from memory. So he finally assumed the task.

In the work Ardo gives only a glimpse of his own life. He was correct when he alluded to his crudity of language: we find, among other matters, employment of accusatives absolute or accusatives mixed with ablatives absolute, prepositions with the wrong case, corrupt forms (*equites* for *equos*, for example). The solecisms, apparent in his latin text, are certainly not unusual for his time and place. He was quite capable of conveying his thoughts adequately, but there is no parade of literary virtuosity. A few references to Virgil appear in his *praefatio* and perhaps at 5:1. Throughout the book occur constant citations of Scripture. Ardo was familiar with the interior life of monastic communities and also with the usual content of saints' lives. But of the latter it is difficult to ascertain with precision any particular ones that he had read.

Ardo claimed personal knowledge both of his subject and of a number of incidents that he had witnessed (e.g., 16; 17; 21.2; 25.3; 28.2; 31.3). Nor did he hesitate to report occasional unfavorable reactions to Benedict. But he had had only fleeting glimpses of the abbot in the great secular world and of Benedict's powerful impact upon it. A single note seems quite revealing: it is a vivid picture which Ardo secured from some source and which contains two items of interest. First is Benedict's procedure when agreeing to intercede with the Emperor for various persons. We observe how modern he was when he caused complaints to be reduced to writing (35.3). Second is the vignette of Louis receiving them. He sat or stood, nervously plucking at his sleeves or a napkin, reading them in order of receipt. When familiarized with the problems presented, Louis rendered judgment as usefully as he could. But sometimes he wearily shoved them aside and forgot them until prodded by Benedict (35.3).

Externally the text of Ardo's *Vita* contains a *praefatio* and forty-one chapters, as well as a collection of three letters and a few notes at the end. Chapter 30, however, is an interpolation dating not earlier than the eleventh century. It purports to be a brief life of William of Gellone. Skillfully constructed to appear an original part of the *Vita Benedicti*, its first sentence ties well to the end of chapter 29.4; the last sentence of 30.5 tries to make transition to chapter 31 easy not by repeating the exact words of 28.2, 'Let us return to the sequence we began', but by adding the word *rurus*, 'Let us *again* return . . .' (30.5). Whoever composed the chapter attempted to convey verisimilitude by one first-personal remark, 'I think it worthwhile to relate . . .' (30.3). The rest of the text bears little relation to the story of Benedict; and moreover, except for one slight allusion (34), Benedict's *Vita* makes no reference to William either before or after the insertion. If chapter 30 is ignored, the flow from the last sentence of chapter 29 to the first of chapter 31 is unbroken.

Apart from that there are inserted thirteen accounts of miracles (12.2; 13; 14; 15; 23; 24.3; 4; 25.3; 26; 27.1; 27.2; 28.1; 31.3, 32). The first four are contiguous and are introduced as miracles, 'Since almighty God . . . performs on suitable occasions miracles through his servants, I will compress into a brief narrative some that he did through Benedict' (12.1). They are concluded with a humorous incident known personally to Ardo (16). The fifth and sixth are fairly contiguous, but not introduced as miracles, only as incidents derived from Ardo's investigations (24.4), the fifth being semi-humorous. The seventh through the eleventh are contiguous and are properly introduced, 'I do not think it amiss if miracles . . . are inserted in this treatment' (25.1); and also concluded, 'Let it suffice to have said these few things about miracles done in our time' (28.2). The twelfth and thirteenth are contiguous, but not introduced or concluded as miracles. It seems therefore apparent that the brothers at Inde had sent along with their letter some appropriate miracle stories involving Benedict and that Ardo felt obliged to use them.

Only seven of them (12.2; 13; 14; 15; 24.3, 4; 31.3; 32) are credited to Benedict himself; the remainder to prayers by all the brothers (23; 26; 27.1; 27.2), to a relic of the cross (25.3), and to presence in a particular oratory (28.1). The last may indeed not be deemed a miracle. Only one of the thirteen (31.3) has the earmarks of a genuine violation of natural law and Ardo told none of these stories with zest. Some he attributed to his own knowledge or investigation (24.3, 4; 25.3, 31.3), not to information provided by another source. He certainly did not rely on them as of importance to the *Vita*.

For dating the *Vita* we have the *terminus a quo* of 821, Benedict's death, and the *terminus ad quem* of 840, the death of Louis the Pious, who is always referred to as living.[55] It must have been no later than 822 when the brothers of Inde collected their notes for Ardo, who

---

55. *Pace* Williams, 'St Benedict of Aniane', 358.

waited a year, thus 823, before accepting the commission. There ensued a period of composition which required time. Consequently, the earliest date for the *Vita* could be 824. In the book there are no allusions to the troubled years of 830-833 when the carolingian court was wracked with intrigue and rebellion[56]—not that the writer had any reason to make such allusions! The biography was, moreover, written while persons who had known Abbot Benedict and his activities were still alive (31.3). Knowing that the pressure on Ardo to write was heavy, it would seem, therefore, appropriate to assign the *Vita* to an interval not earlier than 824 and not later than 830.

But it is possible to narrow the period to 824–826. Ermoldus Nigellus's poem in honor of Emperor Louis may be dated about 827[57] and it seems entirely possible, even likely, that Ermoldus alluded to Ardo's *Vita*. The poem's description of Benedict has been denominated 'stereotyped', conveying 'to the mind little that can be called characteristic'.[58] It does indeed make numerous literary allusions, duly indicated by Ernst Dümmler in his edition.[59] Yet no one can question the aptness of the language despite its borrowings: it is as though Ermoldus had read Ardo's *Vita* and tried to improve its terminology. Just as an example, line 533, *Vir Benedictus erat cognomine dignus eodem* (Benedict was a man worthy of his name), has in it two scarcely significant words, *cognomine dignus*, annotated as from Ovid, *Ex Ponto*, II, 5, 49. In spirit, however, as well as in words, it is similar to Ardo, *Vir venerabilis nomine et merito Benedictus* (The venerable man by name and merit Benedict— that is, 'blessed one', 1.1).[60]

---

56. See The anonymous Life of Louis, III. 44, 45, 48-53, in Cabaniss, *Son of Charlemagne*, 89-92, 95-105 (as in note 3 above).

57. See note 18 above. Ermoldus's poem in four books was edited by Ernst Dümmler in PLAC 2:5-79; a later edtion and translation, *Ermold le Noir, Poème sur Louis le Pieux et épitres au roi Pepin,* was prepared by Edmond Faral (Paris: Champion, 1932). Manitius, *Geschichte*, 554f., contains some useful bibliography.

58. M. L. W. Laistner, *Thought and Letters in Western Europe, A.D. 500 to 900*, 2nd ed. (Ithaca, New York: Cornell University Press, 1957; first published 1931) 356.

59. See note 57 above. My internal citations are from the PLAC edition.

60. Ardo may also have had in mind the opening line of Gregory the Great's *Life of Benedict: Fuit vir vitae venerabilis gratia Benedictus et nomine*—ed.

Ermoldus's line 535, *Hic erat in Geticis regi prius agnitus*[61] *arvis* (He was known[62] in 'Getic' fields before the king), annotated by citation of Vergil, *Aeneid*, III,35, *Geticus qui praesidet arvis* (He who presides over 'Getic' fields), and Ovid, *Ex ponto*, I, 9, 45, *Geticis* . . . *ab arvis* (from 'Getic' fields), is simply a 'glamorised' version of Ardo, *Benedictus abbas ex Getarum genere partibus Gotiae oriundus* (Abbot Benedict was sprung from the nation of 'Getae' in the areas of Gothia, 1.1). Line 536, *De cuius vita pauca referre libet* (It is appropriate to relate a few things about his life) is glossed with two words from Vergil, *Aeneid*, IV, 333, *pauca refert* (he relates a few things), hardly a significant allusion, being so commonplace (this verse will, however, be adverted to again below). Line 546, *regula cuius erat pectore fixa sacro* (whose *Rule* was fixed in his holy breast), perhaps related verbally to Ovid, *Metamorphoses*, VI, 227, *medioque in pectore fixa* (and fixed in the midst of his breast), is another example of an 'improvement' of Ardo, *quo memoire Regula praefati patris commendavit* (where he committed to memory the *Rule* of the aforesaid Father, 2:6).

Other important lines from Ermoldus's poem have no classical overtones, but seem to be directly from Ardo. In line 538 the word *abba* (instead of *abbas*) is used; so also at three points in the *Vita*: 32, 35.2, and 37.2, each time with the adjective *venerabilis*. In my translation, to differentiate it from *abbas* (which I render *abbot*), I have retained the Aramaic *abba* to call attention to it. In line 541 Ermoldus used three nouns to describe Benedict, *fuit* . . . *norma exemplumque magister* (he was . . . a standard, an example, and a teacher). Precisely those three words were also employed by Ardo: *norma* (18.1; 33; 36.2); *exemplum* (36.1); and *magister* (20; 24:3).

Ermoldus's line 588 speaks of the abbey of Inde as *nomen aquae retinens* (keeping the name of the stream); Ardo phrased it thus, *mutuato de rivulo eiusdem vallis nomen* (the name of the valley itself . . . derived from the little river, 35.2). According to line 589 of Ermoldus, who knew the locale, *Milibus hic ternis regali destat ab aula* (It was three miles from the royal palace); Ardo, who did not know the locale, observed, *Vallis autem erat vicina, quae a palatio (ut reor) sex non amplius milibus distat* (There was a neighboring valley which is, *I think*, not more than six

---

61. Although not supported by any MS, this word could be *agnatus* (born). In any case Benedict was born about eighteen years before Louis the Pious.
62. See preceding note.

miles from the palace, 35.2—emphasis added).[63] Ermoldus's line 598 is especially interesting, *Hludowicus adest Caesar et abba* (Louis is present as both emperor and *abba*—or 'abbot'). The monks recorded that, after Benedict's death and even as they were writing, Louis *abbatem se monasterii illius palam esse profietur* (openly declared himself *abba*—or 'abbot'—of that monastery, that is, Inde, 42.2. The words *abba* and *abbas* can have the same accusative, *abbatem*). Ermoldus stated in line 580, *Hoc mandarentur menbra sepulta loco* (that his body would be ordered buried in this place); Ardo included a note from the brothers of Inde that Benedict was interred in a stone coffin *quod imperator paraverat* (that the emperor had had prepared, 42.5).

Let us now return to Ermoldus's line 536, cited above. There it was deliberately given a neutral translation so as not to prejudge the case before evidence was presented. But in view of the relation between Ermoldus's lines and Ardo's treatment, and in view of the strong possibility that Ermoldus knew Ardo's work, I suggest that a more accurate version would be, 'It is appropriate to mention a few things from his [Benedict's] *Vita*'.

WILLIAM OF GELLONE

For the purpose of this treatment of Benedict of Aniane, it is not necessary to add to the extensive literature on William of Gellone. For our purpose indeed it would be better to ignore the interpolated Chapter 30. But some comments are perhaps in order simply to acknowledge a problem. The latest study in English is A.J. Zuckerman, *A Jewish Princedom*, already mentioned in the notes. It relies heavily on Pükert, *Aniane und Gellone*,[64] and Tisset, *L'Abbaye de Gellone*.[65] There are also some sections of Bedier, *Les legendes épiques*, I,[66] that contribute to the subject. But I restrict my remarks to the presentation by Zuckerman as embodying the others. His book is, by the way, quite impressive, but at the time

63. Williams, 'St Benedict of Aniane', 357, 'some eight miles'.

64. Wilhelm Pückert, *Aniane und Gellone* (Leipzig: Hinrichs'che Buchandlung, 1899), especially Chapters 1, 3, and 4.

65. On Tisset (note 25 above), especially Chapters 1, 2, and 5.

66. Joseph Bedier, *Les legendes épiques: recherches sur la formation des chansons de geste,* I, *Le cycle de Guillaume d'Orange*, 3rd ed. (Paris: Édouard Champion, 1926) especially Chapters 3, 4, and 5.

of this writing[67], it has not yet received the close consideration that is due to it.[68] Perhaps that will come in time.

Some elements of the description of William of Gellone in the interpolated chapter, although late, are based on authentic material. He was described by the writer as an eminent and favorite court official of Charles (30.1). About 846, twenty-five years after William's death, Paschasius Radbertus characterized him as 'a most noble and high-minded man' and mentioned that Abbot Wala (*c.* 773–834) was at one time his son-in-law.[69] At some point William became a profound admirer of Benedict (30.1). He was indeed of noble origin (30.2), related to Charles and Louis, but the precise kinship is disputed.[70] The traditional date of his conversion is given as 29 June [806], the feast of Saints Peter and Paul (30.1).[71]

Some problems suggested by Zuckerman[72] can be disposed of quickly. (1) There is no inner contradiction in the assertion, 'with the aid of his sons whom he had set over (*praefecerat*) his counties' (30.3).[73] Note the pluperfect tense: obviously William 'had set' his sons before he himself made any renunciations.

(2) Zuckerman's similarities between the monastic lives of Benedict and William are commonplaces in biographies of saints and require no extended demonstration.[74] (3) Benedict's observance of both the Sabbath (Saturday) and the Lord's Day (Sunday) (21.2) simply reflect his documented attachment to eastern practices where both days were (and are) liturgically commemorated.[75] In fact, the western church also ob-

67. The Introduction was first published in 1979—ed.

68. See reviews by Bernard S. Bachrach, *American Historical Review* (December 1973) 1440f., and by Allen Cabaniss, *Catholic Historical Review* (July 1973) 317–319.

69. Paschasius Radbertus, *Vita Walae*, II. 8,4, as translated in Allen Cabaniss, *Charlemagne's Cousins* (Syracuse: Syracuse University Press, 1967) 161.

70. Probably the most extensive treatment in Joseph Calmette, *De Bernardo s. Guillelmi filio (?–844)* (Toulouse: Privat, 1902) *passim*. But see also Léonce Auzias, *L'Aquitaine carolingienne (778–987)* (Paris: Didier, 1937) 37; Zuckerman, *A Jewish Princedom* (note 20 above), 122, 184; E. Hlawitschka, 'Die Vorfahren Karls des Grossen', in Braunfels, *Karl der Grosse* (note 24 above), 1:51–82, especially 77.

71. The year is given in *Chronicon Moissiacense* (note 6 above).

72. Bibliographical details in note 17 above.

73. Zuckerman, *A Jewish Princedom*, 207, note 82.

74. *Ibid.*, 208 and note 84, citing and adding to Pückert, *Aniane und Gellone* (note 45 above), 109, note 8.

75. Zuckerman, 211.

served (and observes) both days; formerly the Saturday Mass was offered in honor of the Blessed Virgin Mary; today the Saturday vigil Mass has the status of Sunday Mass. Moreover, most Romance languages adopted the medieval and liturgical latin term for Saturday, *sabbatum*; for example, Spanish *sábado* and French *samedi*.

(4) Benedict maintained his abstinence from quadruped meat even in illness: it was a chicken broth (*ius e pullo compositum*, 21:2), not a *beef* broth, that he allowed himself.[76] (5) It was Louis the Pious, not William, who endowed Gellone with 'silver and gold chalices and vessels for the offertory' (30.4).[77] (6) Benedict was hardly 'in flight' from Saint Seine to another monastery:[78] 'he hurriedly set out toward his paternal soil' (3.1) to avoid election as abbot of Saint Seine, a not infrequent occurrence during the Middle Ages. (7) It is not so obvious that he was 'without possessions comparable to' those of William,[79] for Ardo remarked that he built Aniane on 'property belonging to his father *and himself*' (3.1; emphasis added).

(8) Hebraisms in any context are the stock in trade of a hagiologist and need not detain us.[80] (9) The 'archaic' word *consul* for a Frankish official was employed about 846 by Paschasius Radbertus long before any 'revival [of the term] in the eleventh century'.[81] Paschasius also used a more 'archaic word, *senator*, a number of times'.[82] (10) The story about a fasting girl in 823–825 made no allusion to 'her confirmation Mass'.[83]

But important questions raised by Zuckerman remain. Six statements in the interpolated chapter are, at least, strange. (a) It remarks that 'Permission to be converted was finally received' (*acceptamque tandem convertendi licentia*, 30.1). Consent by the ruler for a great noble to become

76. *Ibid.* My rendering is sustained by Williams, 'St Benedict of Aniane', 364. Similar faulty proofreading by Zuckerman occurs on pp. 243f., where he has *Bernard* instead of the correct *Benedict*; see note 96 below.
77. Zuckerman, 212.
78. *Ibid.*
79. *Ibid.*
80. *Ibid.*, 223.
81. *Ibid.*, 224, note 115; but see Paschasius, *Vita Walae*, II, 6:1; 19:1 (Cabaniss, *Charlemagne's Cousins*, 157, 192).
82. Paschasius, *Vita Walae*, I 3:5; 6:5; II, 1:2; 9:7; 15:4 (Cabaniss, *Charlemagne's Cousins*, 93, 100, 149, 167, 182).
83. Zuckerman, *A Jewish Princedom*, 240, note 148; see Allen Cabaniss, 'Popular Revolt in the Ninth Century', *Studies in English*, XIII (1972) 111–118.

a monk was not unusual at that time, but the statement is followed by
(b) William's gift of extensive treasure to Benedict, (c) his hasty tonsure
(*nec mora*), (d) his putting off cloth-of-gold vesture, (e) then his acceptance of 'the habit of Christians' (*Christisticolarum*), and lastly (f) his
expression of gratitude that he was now numbered with the company
of 'heaven-dwellers' (*caelicolarum*) (30.1). When Benedict, who was also
of noble origin, became a monk, there was no mention of any 'permission to be converted', only 'permission to enter', granted by the community of Saint Seine (2.2). Then followed his tonsure, not hastily, as in
the case of William, but in due course (*mox*). And it was said that he
assumed 'the vesture of a true monk' (*veri monachi abitum*, 2.2). Despite
similarities, the two accounts are notably different.

- Permission was for two different aspects of a new life.
- The source of consent for William is not indicated, as it is for
  Benedict.
- In one case the tonsure was hurried; in the other, given apparently
  after a suitable interval.
- The 'habit' of each is differently described, the more ordinary
  expression being for that of Benedict.

The latin word for 'Christians' in the William chapter is *christicolae*,
not *Christiani*. Both latin words were occasionally employed to signify
monks, as also was the term 'heaven-dwellers' (*caelicolarum*), although the
latter could quite naturally mean 'angels'. Those words appear nowhere
else in Ardo's *Vita*, but both occurred in the famed Saint Gall trope
Quem-quaeritis near the end of the ninth century,[84] and there the former
meant 'Christian', the latter, 'angels'. In connection with William it is
entirely possible that the two words were introduced for the sake of an
internal prose rhyme:

> christicolarum induit abitum seseque
> caelicolarum adscisci numero . . . (30.1).

---

84. See too the amusing 'tale of Abbot John' by Fulbert, bishop of Chartres (*fl.*
1007), about the monk who wanted to live *sicut angelus* (like an angel), but repented
after a week of effort; *cum angelus non potuit, vir bonus esse didicit* (since he could not
be an angel, he learned how to be a good man). F. J. E. Raby, ed., *The Oxford Book of
Medieval Latin Verse*, 2nd ed. (Oxford: Clarendon Press, 1959) 180–182.

In fact the concatenation of the rhyming words may be reminiscent of, hence later than, and perhaps influenced by, the trope.

We may now propose the following theses.

1. Permission in Benedict's case was to enter a particular monastic community; in William's case it was to a new life style. Note the use of the word *anastrophe* (manner of life) in the New Testament (Gal 1:13, Eph 4:22; 1 Tim 4:12; Heb 12:7); in every instance it is translated in the Vulgate by the latin word *conversatio*. Ardo used the related word *conversio* as a synonym (21.1) and so did the Benedictine *Rule*. We may at this point add that 'Christian' became in the course of time an occasional *name* for a person converted to Christianity from Islam or Judaism.[85]

2. Permission to Benedict was granted by the monastery of Saint Seine; to William it was granted either by the frankish emperor *or by a circle to which William formerly belonged*.

3. For Benedict taking the tonsure was voluntary and orderly (*comam deposuit*), but for William it did not appear to be an entirely free act (*nec mora in deponendo comam fieri passus est*); observe the passive quality of the assertion and the fact that he 'suffered it to be done'.

4. Benedict's habit was the usual monastic garb. Was William's habit, that 'of Christians', in this instance therefore, baptismal?

I suggest that the account of William's 'conversion' in Chapter 30, however muted, constituted an astounding event in the carolingian world, comparable to the opposite conversion of Bodo, a Christian court chaplain, into Eleazar, an active Jewish propagandist in Muslim Spain.[86] This assumption tends to explain Florenz of Wevelinkhofen's fourteenth-century mention of William's conversion from Christianity to Judaism, then back to Christianity.[87] He was clearly in error about William's conversion to Judaism, the remark is probably a conflation with the Bodo-Eleazar affair. Zuckerman is right in supposing that 'it hardly would have been possible for a Jewish convert from Christianity to remain at court . . . or within reach of the authorities'.[88] But that *Jews as*

---

85. Urban T. Holmes, Jr., in Holmes and M. Amelia Klenke, *Chrétien, Troyes, and the Grail* (Chapel Hill, N.C.: University of North Carolina Press, 1959), 51–61.

86. See Cabaniss, 'Bodo-Eleazar' (note 14 above).

87. Cited by Zuckerman, *A Jewish Princedom*, 238–241.

88. *Ibid.*, 241.

such could do so, and in fact did, is evident. They were a highly respected minority with powerful influence.[89] William as a Jew by birthright (if Zuckerman's evidence is accepted) could be and was held in lofty esteem. By turning to Christianity (perhaps, although not certainly, to monasticism), William created a furor among both Jews and Christians comparable to that raised in a similar way by Bodo-Eleazar later, the vague memory of which was later exploited by Florenz of Wevelinkhofen.

We can accept Zuckerman's comments as apt: 'The conclusion appears inescapable that no authentic contemporary document reports William's assumption of the monastic habit. This is altogether a fabrication dating no earlier than the eleventh century'.[90] But Zuckerman neglected his best internal evidence: he did not make anything of a very ambiguous passage in the interpolation which noted that William, although dedicating himself wholly to Christ, did not abandon any 'trace of worldly ostentation' (*nichil mundanae pompae relinquens vestigium*, 30.4).[91]

We must now revert to the issue of the source of William's 'permission to be converted'. Was it from the jewish community or from his frankish political superiors? It is worth recalling that Bodo-Eleazar secured no permission from either source. But William was a loyal subject of the Frankish ruler. It is, of course, possible that he first discussed conversion with his Jewish confrères, but it is much more likely that as an eminent landed nobleman he required permission from his secular ruler for 'any great or important undertaking', even baptism, involving as it did a change of life style. One may account for the conversion of William on prudential grounds, perhaps to insure that his property would go to his sons, perhaps in some way to protect them. It is significant that his most famous son was baptized with Louis the Pious standing as sponsor.[92]

---

89. See Cabaniss, *Agobard of Lyons*, 63–71 (note 42 above).

90. Zuckerman, *A Jewish Princedom*, 242.

91. The Latin is ambiguous: it may be read as above or as, 'leaving behind no trace of worldly ostentation'. Logic virtually demands this latter version, which is rendered in French by Bedier, *Les legendes épiques* 1:113 (as in note 66 above): '. . . sans plus garder aucun vestige des pompers mondaines'. Grammatically and verbally the reading given in the text above is not only possible, but also probable. What it really means, I do not know, but compare the unambiguous statement in 35.2: *seculari pompa relicta* (secular pomp abandoned).

92. Thegan, *Vita Hludowici*, 36, in Reinhold Rau, *Fontes ad historiam regni Francorum aevi Karolini illustrandam,* 1 (Berlin: Rütten und Loening, 1956) 236.

Here we are led to accept two further corrections made by Zuckerman in the traditional accounts. First, his suggestion that Bernard, William's
son, was born about 806 is surely appropriate.[93] I had already reached a
like conclusion about fifteen years before Zuckerman's book appeared.[94]
Second, his presumption that William did not die before 814, but 'closer
to 822',[95] 'around the reputed date of death of the monk [Benedict] of
Aniane',[96] makes for a better understanding of the material before us,
although the date was anticipated several years before Zuckerman by
David Knowles.[97]

93. Zuckerman, *A Jewish Princedom*, 217, note 98.

94. See Allen Cabaniss, 'France's First Woman of Letters', in *Judith Augusta* (note
7 above), 52; originally published as 'The Woes of Dhuoda' in *Mississippi Quarterly*
11:1 (Winter 1958) 38-49.

95. Zuckerman, 239, note 144.

96. *Ibid.*, 244. Here and on the preceding page Zuckerman mistakenly substi-
tuted the name *Bernard* for *Benedict*.

97. Knowles, *From Pachomius to Ignatius* (note 11 above), 8.

TRANSLATOR'S ACKNOWLEDGMENTS

There appears to be no previous vernacular translation of the full Ardo, *Vita Benedicti*, only of small portions; and little effort has been made to provide a narrative account of Benedict's life. There are some cursory remarks about him in Eleanor S. Duckett, *Alcuin, Friend of Charlemagne* (New York: Macmillan, 1951), and her *Carolingian Portraits* (Ann Arbor: University of Michigan Press, 1962), but nothing much beyond a summary of Ardo's *Vita*. So far as I know, there has been no successor comparable to P.J. Nicolai, *Der heilige Benedict, Gründer von Aniane und Cornelimünster, Reformator des Benedictinerordens* (Cologne, 1865), which was not available to me (the Library of Congress being authority for the assertion that it is not in the United States).[1] Most later treatments deal with specialized aspects of Benedict's life and activities, but that is not my purpose here.

My procedure has been to make the translation and write [the first two] sections of the introduction before consulting any secondary material in order to arrive at a fresh, uninhibited consideration of the subject. Only then did I turn to comments by others. The notes will indicate my indebtedness, but I must single out for special mention the following:

- Sigurd Abel, *Jahrbücher des fränkischen Reichs unter Karl dem Grossen*, 2 volumes: Vol. I, 2nd ed. Bernhard Simson. Leipzig: Duncker und Humblot, 1888; Vol. 2, completed by Simson in 1883.

1. The Library of Congress was unaware of a copy in the library of Gethsemani Abbey in Kentucky. It is now on permanent loan in the Rare Book Room of Waldo Library at Western Michigan University, Kalamazoo.

- Bernard S. Bachrach, 'A Reassessment of Visigothic Jewish Policy, 589–711', *American Historical Review*, 78:1 (February 1973) 11–34; review of Zuckerman (see below), *ibid.*, No. 5 (December 1973) 1440f.
- Joseph Bédier, *Les legendes épiques: recherches sur la formation des chansons de geste,* I, *Le cycle de Guillaume d'Orange,* 3ʳᵈ ed. Paris: Édouard Champion, 1926, especially Chapters 3, 4, and 5.
- J. F. Böhmer, E. Mühlbacher, J. Lechner, *Die Regesten des Kaiserreichs unter den Karolingern 751–918.* Innsbruck:Verlag der Wagner'schen Universitäts-Buchhandlung, 1908.
- Erich Bornmann, *Zeitrechnung und Kirchenjahr* and *Calendarium perpetuum.* Kassel: Johannes Stauda, 1964.
- Wolfgang Braunfels, ed., *Karl der Grosse: Lebenswerk und Nachleben,* Vols. I–IIII (1965), IV (1967), V (indexes, 1968). Düsseldorf: L. Schwann. See especially Philippe Wolff, 'L'Aquitaine et ses marges', 1:269–321; Wilhelm Heil, 'Der Adoptianismus, Alkuin und Spanien', 2:95-155; Joseph Semmler, 'Karl der Grosse und das fränkische Mönchtum', 2:255-289, embodying the results of some of his earlier essays.
- J. Calmette, De Bernardo sancti Guillelmi filio (?–844). Toulouse: Privat, 1902.
- Charles W. Jones, *Saints' Lives and Chronicles in Early England.* Ithaca, New York: Cornell University Press, 1947.
- Max Manitius, Geschichte der lateinischen Literatur des Mittelalters, 1.I Munich: Beck, 1911.
- Wilhelm Pückert, *Aniane und Gellone.* Leipzig, Hinrichs'che Buchhandlung, 1899.
- Pierre Tisset, *L'Abbaye de Gellone au diocèse de Lodéve des origines au XIIIe siècle.* Paris: Recueil Sirey, 1933.
- Watkin Williams, 'St Benedict of Aniane', *Downside Review,* 54 (July 1936) 357–374.
- J. Winandy, 'L'Oeuvre monastique de saint Benoît d'Aniane', *Mélanges bénédictines* (Saint Wandrille, 1947) 235–258.
- Arthur J. Zuckerman, *A Jewish Princedom in Feudal France 768–900.* New York: Colulmbia University Press, 1972.
- *Corpus consuetudinum monasticarum,* 1: 501–536, 'Regula sancti Benedicti abbatis Anianensis sive Collection capitularis', and 563–582,

'Modus penitentiarum Benedicti abbatis Anianensis', both edited by J. Semmler. Siegburg: F. Schmitt, 1963.

My thanks go to Winston W. Way, Jr., a graduate student at Michigan State University, who drew my special attention to the subject; as always to my sister, Frances C. Stephens, who helped me with proofing, indexing, and listening to early drafts; and to my little great-nephew Bobby, Junior (to whom this book is affectionately dedicated), for frequently distracting me with his playfulness. And since this final paragraph is already sentimental, I must add still another acknowledgment: to a dear old cat that was with me for more than twenty years. Carolota (named for both Charlemagne and the ill-fated Mexican empress) often lay in my lap purring as I wrote or sprawled beside my typewriter as I copied my work; her memory haunts me yet.

A.C.

University, Mississippi
Solemnity of Our Lady of Guadalupe, 1978

EOITOR'S NOTE

The editors of Cistercian Publications express their deep appreciation to Elizabeth Orsburn of Oxford, Mississippi, the niece of Allen Cabaniss, for giving us permission to publish a new edition of this translation and to include it and Professor Cabaniss' introduction in the Cistercian Studies Series as the first of an on-going sub-series on reforming monks during the european Middle Ages. For the sake of consistency among these *Lives*, and to bring the translation into conformity with the editorial policies of Cistercian Publications, some few slight changes have been made to the translation. The most notable of these is the use of 'Christ', rather than 'Messiah', to translate the Latin *Christus*. Professor Cabaniss' reasons for using 'Messiah' are explained in his Introduction. After considerable reflection, the editors decided that since Ardo used the Latin form familiar to his contemporaries, the translation should employ the equivalent word most familiar to English-speakers today.

The base text used for the translation is *Vita sancti Benedicti Anianensis et Indensis abbatis,* edited by Georg Waitz and published in the series Monumenta Germaniae Historia: Scriptores, volume 15/1, pages 200–220. The text is also found in the Patrologia Latina, volume 101, columns 353–384. In the years since Professor Cabaniss first published his translation, vernacular translations in French and German have appeared, and his own translation, originally published in England by Arthur H. Stockwell, Ltd, Ilfracombe, Devon (1979) has been incorporated into Thomas F. X. Noble and Thomas Head, edd., *Soldiers of Christ. Saints and Saints' Lives from Late Antiquity and the Early Middle Ages.* (University Park: Pennsylvania State University Press, 1995) 213–254. The french translation, *Ardon. Vie de Benoît d'Aniane,* Vie monastique.,

Série Monachisme ancien 39 Introduction et notes par Pierre Bonnerue, traduit de F. Baumes, revisé et corrigé par Adalbert de Vogüé, was published in 2001 by the Abbaye de Bellefontaine, and is also available on-line as part of a library of electronic monastic texts provided by the Abbey of Saint-Benoît de Port-Valais, Switzerland at http://www.abbaye-saint-benoit.ch/saints/aniane/benoitaniane.htm. A German translation with facing Latin text has been prepared by students of Professor Dr Gerhard Schmitz of Tübingen University, and this is also available on-line, with a continually updated bibliography of secondary works, at http://www.rotula.de/aniane/text/index.htm. The editors are grateful to Professor Schmitz for recommending two of his graduate students to write a new foreword which shares in English some of the scholarship this Tübingen group has surveyed and the conclusions they have reached. We are also grateful to Annette Grabowsky and Clemens Radl, who took on the task of incorporating their research and insights into a succinct Foreword and for completing it in a remarkably short span of time. Finally, but far from least, we are grateful to Marvin Döbler of Bayreuth University for bringing the Tübingen link to our attention, and to Dr Cornelia Oefelein, who translated the Foreword, also in a very short time.

Cistercian Publications hopes that the reappearance of Professor Cabaniss' translation will spur English-speaking scholars to look again at Carolingian monasticism and its reforming monks, and remind Cistercian readers of the long tradition of monastic reform on which their founders built, even while, in some details, rejecting their decisions.

ERE

THE LIFE OF
BENEDICT OF ANIANE
BY
ARDO

PREFACE

TO THE VENERABLE masters, fathers and brothers, serving God Jesus at the monastery of Inde, Ardo,[1] slave of Christ's servants, sends greeting.

A long time ago, my dearly beloved brothers, your letters were delivered to me, letters full of love for the pious memory of our Father Abbot Benedict. They contained briefly but lovingly an account of his death and departure to Christ. In them you deigned to suggest to my littleness[2] that I write more elaborately for those who want to hear about the beginning of his manner of life. Thus far, however, I have demurred, being aware of the burden on my abilities.

If only by perceptive zeal care could be taken by those composing a life of persons who went before—a life respected for merits and famed for virtues—not to overlook profitable matters when led to do so by partiality; if they could write with fluent pen only matters scrupulously ascertained and confirmed by report of trustworthy witnesses, they would not embarrass the ears of scholars by offering the blemish of inelegance.[3] They would present words savoring of witty urbanity and with polished language titillate the ears of detractors.

---

1. On Ardo, see the Introductory section on, THE AUTHOR AND THE TEXT. I have bypassed the possibility that Ardo may also have been known as Smaragdus, not to be confused with Smaragdus of Saint-Mihiel, a later person of that name.

2. The oldest *Life of Saint Gregory the Great,* by a monk of Whitby, alludes (III) to 'our small ability'. See Charles W. Jones, *Saints' Lives and Chronicles in Early England* (Ithaca, N.Y.: Cornell University Press, 1947) 118.

3. Sulpicius Severus, *Life of Saint Martin, Bishop of Tours,* in the dedication expresses fear that unpolished diction might prove displeasing to a reader. See F. R. Hoare, *The Western Fathers* (New York: Sheed and Ward, 1954) 10.

But conscious of my shortcomings, I have long maintained silence even though persuaded to acquiesce in your request. I have refrained so that it might be expressed by more learned persons, believing that it was surely unfair for me with inept verbiage to touch the life of so great a patron. I have deferred the appropriate task to more skillful writers. With flowing supply of words they can make clear (and even with a flourish) whatever they wish, since they have nothing to fear. They can steer the vessel between the sandbanks[4] and avoid the bad odor of grammatical errors. Gifted with facility of language they have that abundance of speech which checks the tongues of detractors.

I was fearful that readers, irritated at what was badly constructed, might seek to correct clumsy composition.[5] They would thus adjudge the content to be ignored, especially since I knew that you were present at the entrance to the sacred hall of the palace, that you thirsted to for drink of boisterous streams, but eagerly drained the flow of wisdom from an unfailing watercourse of the purest fountain. Such reasoning restrained me for the space of a year.

In the meanwhile you, brothers, undertook to rouse my lethargic inclination with stinging words, you brothers whom with holy endeavor Benedict begot for Christ. You constrained me to bring him to life for you by tales[6] of his life in religion. It is certain that you are absent from him only in fellowship with his bodily presence, not in fullness of charity. So I am finally about to unfold a composition. Even the place—originally erected by him—and the brothers—who knew the beginning of his way of life—have given me a bold and favorable purpose. For what to some can scarcely be unheard, can by them hardly be unseen. Since the materials have been comprehensively assembled, we are ready to disclose more elaborately those that are suitable for the task. We severely confine as it were a seedbed as we are about to publish it more widely.

We humbly beg that if anyone find this work distasteful he will leave it alone or correct it.[7] Otherwise he may allow others to read and study

4. Perhaps vague Vergilian allusions.

5. Sulpicius, *Saint Martin,* dedication (Hoare, *Western Fathers,* 10), asks readers to pay attention to matter rather than to language.

6. *gestis*: see 38.3; 41.1 below. Cf. Paschasius Radbertus, *Adalard,* 2; 4.2; *Wala,* I, 5.4, 5, 6 (Cabaniss, *Charlemagne's Cousins,* 26f., 96f.).

7. Sulpicius, *Saint Martin,* dedication, as in note 3 above.

it while he turns himself to reading the life[8] of earlier fathers. But if he should find that this man did not stray from their path and influence, let him be glad. If he must refute it, let it not be a hasty judgment. Let him interrupt himself and refer it tearfully to the just and peaceful Judge.

Since I have obeyed your request, holy brothers, I ask you to aid me by prayers to God, for pardon of my faults, and for future readers to make progress by reading this book.[9] I beg you to read it with watchful zeal. Correct in detail whatever you may show to be in error. If there are useful matters in it, cherish them in the secret of your breast. By removing the force of silence we have at your command provided a mood, if not an outward act. But you must attribute our speaking to yourselves, remembering that you compelled us to break silence.[10]

Abbot Helisachar[11] clung to Benedict with a disposition of unique love as he left this world—so the abbot's letter, more precious than gold, addressed to us bears witness.[12] For that reason, after you have examined this book, I think it should be presented to him in particular. Should he decide for it to be suppressed, I beg forgiveness for my error.[13] But should he deem it useful, let those who freely obeyed Benedict when he was alive, now devote themselves to imitating his life although he is absent.

Every scholar knows, I suppose, that there is a very ancient custom, still practiced by kings, for matters that are done or events that occur to be committed to annals for the information of future generations. The mind becomes blind to various happenings when forgetfulness supervenes. We therefore believe it divinely planned for things to be preserved in records so that obliging forgetfulness and scurrying time may not efface them. Those who desire to read such chronicles take pleasure in them. They are gladdened and they turn themselves to

8. We today would employ the plural, but medieval writers stressed the singular; see Gregory of Tours, *Liber vitae patrum*, SS. rer. Merow, 1:662f.

9. Sulpicius, *Saint Martin,* preface (Hoare, *Western Fathers,* 10), to rouse a desire for true wisdom.

10. *Ibid.*, dedication (Hoare, *Western Fathers,* 10), when asked so often, the author cannot refuse.

11. Abbot of Saint Riquier and imperial chancellor; see the introduction.

12. See below 41.4; 43.1-4.

13. Sulpicius, *Saint Martin,* dedication (Hoare, *Western Fathers,* 10).

expressions of gratitude. An author of such a record is not judged rash by them even if it does not resound with polished words and even if an avid reading of it may require great exertion.

Let them agree with us both to read the life of those going before us and to entrust to posterity what in our own times we have seen or heard, so as to spur souls on to progress. Let us who emit the odor of crudity not be condemned for unskilled language. We deem it sufficient to draw forth a salutary patter albeit with rude words and to exhibit delicious honey in rough honeycombs. Let each one take by his own choice what he finds acceptable to his mind.

ÞERE BEGINS TÞE LIFE

CHAPTER ONE

1. That venerable man, by name and merit Abbot Benedict, was sprung from the nation of the Getae [Goths] in the area of Gothia.[14] Born of noble origin he was, but heavenly religion ennobled him by even greater brilliance of character. His father held the county of Maguelonne as long as he lived. With all his might he was utterly loyal to the nation of Franks.[15] He was courageous and clever, and to enemies very dangerous. With vast slaughter, as everyone knows, he overthrew the Basques who entered the frontiers of the Frankish realm to lay it waste. None escaped except one whom precipitate flight spared. He entrusted his aforesaid son, while still in boyhood years, to the court of glorious King Pepin to be brought up amid the queen's scholars. Bearing his age with natural quality of mind, Benedict was beloved by his comrades in arms.[16] He was of nimble wit and adaptable in everything. Later he received the office of cupbearer. He performed military service in the days of the aforesaid king. After the latter's death and the accession of most glorious King Charles,[17] Benedict was attached to him in service.

2. In the meanwhile divine grace enlightened him. He began to blaze with heavenly love to abandon this flaming world with all its exertions[18]

14. Southern France. See Introduction, above page 29.

15. Sulpicius, *Saint Martin*, II (Hoare, *Western Fathers*, 12), his father, beginning life as common soldier, rose to the office of military tribune.

16. *Ibid.*, II (Hoare, 14), won the hearts of his fellow soldiers.

17. *Ibid.*, II (Hoare, 13), was a cavalryman under Emperor Justinian and later under Caesar Julian.

18. Cp. Felix, *Life of Saint Guthlac*, 33 (Jones, *Saints' Lives* [note 2], 141), 'our athlete of Christ'.

and to shun that perishable honor which, he realized, one could attain with effort, but once gained could quickly lose. Brooding over this in his heart for a period of three years, he kept it secret except from God. He continued to associate himself in body, though not in mind, with activities of the world.[19] During that interval he tried to grasp the pinnacle of continence, to deprive his body of sleep, to check his tongue, to abstain from food, to take wine sparingly, and to prepare himself like a skilled athlete[20] for future struggle. While still in secular habit he pondered those matters he afterwards fulfilled with devotion.

3. Although he wanted to divest himself of activities of the world, he hesitated about the ways in which that could be done: whether to assume the habit of a pilgrim, or perhaps to attach himself to someone to take care of men's sheep and cattle without pay, or even to engage in the shoemaker's craft in some city and spend on poor folk whatever profit he might be able to gain. While his mind was vacillating in such debate, he turned himself to love of life under the Rule.

CHAPTER TWO

1. In the year that Italy was made subject to the sway of glorious King Charles, Benedict's brother, while he sought recklessly to ford a certain river, was caught up in the swelling waves. Benedict, sitting on his horse, perceived his brother's peril, and plunged headlong into the flood to rescue the drowning exile from danger. As his horse swam forward Benedict grasped his brother's hand. The brother took hold and held on desperately. He who wanted to rescue the drowning man barely escaped death's danger.[21] Then and there Benedict bound himself by a vow to God not to serve the world any further. He returned to his homeland but did not tell his father about his intention.

2. Now there was a certain man of religion named Widmar who lacked bodily sight, but shone in his heart with light. To him Benedict

19. Sulpicius, *Saint Martin*, 3 (Hoare, 15), Martin continued in his military service, but only in name, for nearly two years after baptism; *Gregory the Great*, 2 (Jones, *Saints' Lives*, 98), thought it better to cling to secular dress.

20. Felix, *Saint Guthlac*, XXXIII (Jones, *Saints' Lives*, 141), 'our athlete of Christ'.

21. It is strange that the author does not reveal whether the attempt was successful.

revealed his desire. Widmar kept the secret and offered salutary counsel. When everything was ready, Benedict undertook a journey as though to go to Aix. But when he reached the house of Saint Seine, he ordered his companions to return to their native country, then announced that he wanted to serve Christ God in that monastery. He thereupon requested permission to enter. When that was obtained, he soon laid aside the hair of his head and put on the habit of a true monk.

3. When Benedict became a monk he proceeded to damage his body with incredible fasting for the space of two years and six months.[22] In that way he was, of course, endangering his own flesh as if it were a bloodthirsty beast. He took scanty food, sustaining his body with bread and water to avert death but not hunger, shunning wine as if it were a noxious poison. When his mind was overpowered and he sought a little sleep, he would rest for a short while by lying down on a cheap quilt.[23] Sometimes prostrate on the bare ground, he rested when totally exhausted, but only in order to fatigue himself even more by such rest.[24] Often spending the whole night in prayer he kept himself awake by standing with bare feet on the pavement in the icy cold. He devoted himself so completely to divine meditation that he would continue many days in sacred psalmody without breaking the rule of silence.

4. While others were asleep he cleaned their shoes with water and oiled them, then returned them to their proper places.[25] Certain of them, alas, like jeering madmen, threw their boots at him as he stood some distance away. Their insane foolishness he endured with lofty serenity and high purpose. In his own clothing he reduced himself with such beggarliness that it was scarcely possible for those, who did not know better, to be persuaded that it was as it appeared. He had a cheap old tunic that he did not change until many days had elapsed.[26] Inevitably a colony of lice grew on his filthy skin, feeding on his limbs emaciated by fasts. His cowls were threadbare with extreme age. When

22. See 3.1; 42.1.

23. Constantius, *Life of Saint Germanus*, 4 (Hoare, *Western Fathers*, 289), only bedclothes were a piece of sacking.

24. *Ibid.*, could get little sleep in such discomfort.

25. Sulpicius, *Saint Martin*, 2 (Hoare, *Western Fathers*, 13), cleaning his servant's boots.

26. Constantius, *Saint Germanus*, 4 (Hoare, *Western Fathers*, 289), garments used, unless one was given away, until they fell apart from wear.

the old threads were finally broken, he patched the rent with any available rag even if of a different color, a fact that rendered him somewhat unsightly.[27] He was, therefore, ridiculed, shoved, spat upon by many people,[28] but his mind, fixed upon heaven, sought even cheaper materials. On festal days, when others put on neater clothes, he wore his old ones without any timidity. During that period he never indulged his body in baths. Yet he employed himself for the cleanliness of the monastery as often as opportunity demanded.

5. The grace of compunction[29] and divine help were granted to him in such large measure that he could weep at will. In fear of Gehenna[30] he was daily sustained by tears and groans as he sang lovingly the Davidic words, 'I ate ashes for bread and mingled my cup with tears'.[31] His face grew gaunt with fasting; his flesh was exhausted by privation; his shriveled skin hung from his bones like the dewlaps of cows. Not so much taming a young but ungovernable animal, as mortifying the body, although he was compelled by the abbot to exercise rigor against himself more sparingly, he gave assent reluctantly. Declaring that the Rule of blessed Benedict was for beginners and weak persons, he strove to climb up to the precepts of blessed Basil and the rule of blessed Pachomius.[32] However much the Benedictine Rule might regulate possible things for paltry people, our Benedict perennially explored more impossible

---

27. *Ibid.*

28. Sulpicius, *Saint Martin*, III (Hoare, *Western Fathers*, 15), laughter from bystanders at his grotesque look in ragged garments.

29. For a definition of compunction, see Grimlaic, *Regula solitariorum*, 29 (PL 103:617D), *Compunctio etenim cordis est humilitas mentis cum lacrymis et recordatione peccatorum et timore judicii* (Compunction of heart is humility of mind together with tears, remembrance of sins, and fear of judgment). See also *ibid.*, 30 (618D): *Duo igitur sunt compunctionum genera hoc est irriguum superius et irriguum inferius. Irriguum quippe inferius accipit cum inferni supplicia flendo pertimescit. Irriguum vero superius accipit cum sese in lacrymis coelestis regni desiderio afflegit* (There are two kinds of compunction, namely, one watered from above; the other, from below. Whoever shudders and weeps at the punishments of hell has the compunction watered from below. But he who melts in tears at desire for the kingdom of heaven has the compunction watered from above).

30. Felix, *Saint Guthlac*, 32 (Jones, *Saints' Lives,* 141), same reference to Gehenna.

31. Ps 102 [Vulgate 101]:10. Constantius, *Saint Germanus*, 3 (Hoare, *Western Fathers,* 288), took a taste of ashes before eating his barley bread.

32. See the Introduction, and Knowles, *From Pachomius to Ignatius*, 3–5.

things. Dedicating himself wholly to penance and lamentation, he could not be imitated by anyone or only by a few. But divine favor decreed that he was to become an example of salvation for many and would be inflamed with love for the Rule of Benedict, and like a new athlete[33] just back from single combat enter the field to fight publicly. In the meanwhile he undertook to correct the manners of some, to scold the negligent, exhort beginners, admonish the upright to Persevere, and upbraid the wicked to turn from their ways.

6. After that it was enjoined upon him to supervise the cellar. There he committed to memory the Rule of the aforesaid Father Benedict. He sought with all his might to comport himself according to its regulations and then without delay to be generous to those seeking lawful things, to deny those seeking in a bad way, and courteously to excuse those inquiring for impossible things. Because he did not freely provide them cups, he was not regarded with favor by many. The care of guests, children, and poor folk he exercised with assiduity.[34] The abbot also esteemed him with supreme fondness, because he was beneficial in everything, circumspect in his own life, solicitous for the salvation of others, prompt in ministering, infrequent in speaking, ready to obey, good-natured in serving. Divine piety conferred on him, among other virtues, the gift of understanding and a supply of spiritual eloquence.

CHAPTER THREE

1. The space of five years and eight months[35] having flown by in salutary activities, the abbot of that monastery departed from the world. With one mind and joint agreement all then chose Benedict to be set over them. But knowing that there was no compatibility between their manner and his, he hurriedly set out toward his paternal soil. There, on property belonging to his father and himself, at the brook called Aniane near the river Saône, he, along with Widmar and a few others, erected for their residence a small hut close to the modest church of Saint Saturinus. For several years he lived there in great poverty. For nights and days he entreated divine clemency with groanings and tears that

33. See note 20 above.
34. This sentence alludes to Chapter 3 of the Benedictine Rule, on the duties of cellarer to the sick, children, guests, and poor.
35. See 2.3 above and 42.1 below.

what he wanted might progress to very powerful effect. At the same time in that province there were certain active men of great holiness, namely, Atilio, Nibridius, and Anianus,[36] living a religious life, but unaware of supervision by a rule. When Benedict became known to them, they held him in high esteem. When adverse influence threatened to overcome him, he would saddle his little donkey quickly and hurry away to Atilio, his nearest neighbor.

2. At first many who abandoned the world attempted to live the religious life with him. But bruised in spirit and afraid of a new manner of life when compelled to embrace an unheard-of way of abstinence, such as receiving bread by weight and wine by measure,[37] they soon retraced the steps along which they once set on the road to salvation, and returned like swine to mire and a dog to his vomit[38]. The man of God observed their unsteady faith and being disturbed, wanted to go back to his own monastery.

3. For that reason Benedict approached Atilio for counsel. When he related his wish, Atilio scolded him, 'It has been revealed to me from heaven that you are given to men as a lamp.[39] It would be fitting for you to complete the good work[40] you have begun. This trouble has come to pass by deceit of the ancient enemy who always grudges, always hates good deeds. No concession should ever be made to him.' Bolstered by Atilio's advice, Benedict fearlessly applied himself with ardent spirit to what he longed to accomplish. Not building upon another's foundation,[41] he began with new endeavor to erect houses as well as to expound the strange new way[42] of salvation.

CHAPTER FOUR

1. After a few brothers assembled about him—indeed they flocked to him when his belief became known—the venerable Benedict began to flourish in holy religion at that place. He freely expounded on the

36. See Introduction, p. 38.
37. See RB 30.4 and 31.4.
38. See 2 Pt 2:22.
39. Acts 13:47.
40. Phil 1:6.
41. Rom 15:20.
42. Acts 17:19f.

heavenly road to those who wanted it and labored with his own hands. Lest as he preached to others he should be found fickle,[43] he took care to fulfill what Atilio had warned him should be pursued. Now, he did not, through fear of want, give up the work he had begun. On the contrary, as the Apostle says, beset by hunger and thirst, in cold and nakedness,[44] he urged his subordinates to persist with untroubled heart, teaching that the way that leads to life is constricted and narrow,[45] that the sufferings of this time are not comparable to future glory that will be revealed to the holy ones.[46] Strengthened by his example, they yearned to be exhausted by even heavier labors.

2. At that time they had no possessions, no vineyards, no cattle, no horses. There was only one small donkey. By its help the weariness of the brothers was relieved when it was necessary for them in turn to travel any distance. They received wine only on Lord's days and festivals. Their hunger was occasionally assuaged with milk brought by neighboring women. They wasted their bodies by dehydration, living only on bread and water. To ward off the constant cold, they used blankets when they attended divine Vigils. They were indeed poor in possessions, but wealthy in merits. The more their bodies were impaired with want, the more their souls were fattened with virtues. They burned with heavenly love; tears alone brought them consolation in their poverty. The ancient foe, observing their unconquered brotherly unity,[47] strove to divide it by craft.

3. They had nearby only one mill in which they ground what provisions they might have. One night a visitor, goaded by malign thoughts, came to them. They made him as comfortable as possible in the donkey's stall. But, watching with evil intent, he got up as soon as they were asleep and left, taking along what he lay on, the jug from which he drank water, and even the tools of the mill, thus repaying evil for good.[48] The next morning the students reported to the master the loss they had discovered. He taught them to endure with good will injuries

43. 1 Cor 9:27.
44. 2 Cor 11:27.
45. Mt 7:14.
46. Rom 8:18.
47. Ps 133 [132]:1.
48. 1 Thess 5:15.

inflicted on them and to consider losses as gain,[49] entreating them rather
to grieve for him who forgot faith while straining to take advantage.

CHAPTER FIVE

1. In the meanwhile the band of students began gradually to increase.
The fame of holy religious observance began by degrees to flit by the
mouths of those dwelling nearby,[50] spreading itself to places a long
distance away. Because the valley in which he had first setttled was very
narrow, he undertook little by little to erect by new effort a monastery
beyond its confines. Sometimes he labored with the brothers as they
worked; sometimes he had his hands full with cooking food for them
to eat, while at the same time he was also occupied even in the kitchen
with writing a book. And often, because of the scarcity of oxen, he
carried wood on his own shoulders along with his students.

2. There was on the place where they were endeavoring to establish
the monastery a building which they expanded and dedicated in honor
of holy Mary the bearer of God. With people flocking thither from
everywhere, begging earnestly to submit themselves to his superinten-
dency, the fabric of the monastery was quickly completed. The place
was endowed and increased with properties as various persons offered
what they had. Benedict had given orders to make the houses, not with
ornate walls, red roof tiles, or painted panelings, but with thatch and
cheap timber. Although the number of brothers was rapidly expanding,
he still strove for rather cheap and modest materials.

3. If anyone wanted to bestow some of his possessions on the monastery, Benedict accepted it. But if someone pressed to attach serving
men and women to it, he refused. Nor did he permit anyone to be
delivered to the monastery by charter, but ordered them to be set free.
He preferred himself that the vessels for Christ's body not be of silver.
To him first choice was wooden vessels, secondly glass, and finally tin.
He refused to have a silken chasuble. If some person gave him one, he
immediately gave it away to others.

49. Phil 3:7f.
50. Cf. Vergil, *Aeneid*, IV, 173–177.

CHAPTER SIX

In the mean time in the same region or thereabout several religious men constructed monasteries and gathered monks, disciplining themselves according to the blessed man's example. Steeped in his instruction, they pruned away their former life and old errors. To them he was like a father, bringing assistance and support not only in spiritual matters, but also in material. Often visiting them he urged them not to abandon the work they had begun lest the spirit, oppressed by want and worn by terrors, look backwards. And so monasteries, sustained by wholesome witness, became numerous and the multitude of monks was at a peak.

CHAPTER SEVEN

1. At the same time a very severe famine occurred.[51] Many poor folk, widows, and orphans began to stream to him and to crowd the gates and roads of the monastery. When he saw them languishing for lack of nourishment, almost swallowed up by death itself, he was troubled because he did not know how he could feed such a number.[52] But since nothing is lacking to those who fear God,[53] whatever new produce they might lay hands on to supply the brothers he ordered to be set aside separately. He then gave command that the rest be distributed each day by designated brothers. Meat of cattle and sheep was given out every day and even goat's milk provided sustenance. They made huts for themselves in suitable places where they could dwell until the new harvests.

2. When food began to fail, Benedict gave another order to measure out what he had commanded to be set aside for the brothers' use. That was done three times. Among the brothers the mood of pity was so strong that they would have weighed out everything if it had been permitted. What each one was entitled to withdraw for himself, he secretly allotted to those consumed with hunger. Even so they were barely rescued from the peril of famine, for several times a man was found dead although there was bread in his mouth.

51. See Introduction, p. 28.
52. Jn 6:5.
53. Jb 8:12.

CHAPTER EIGHT

1. I do not think one should maintain silence when at nearly the same time the baneful doctrine of Felicianism invaded that province.[54] Un-harmed by the noxious error of unbelief, Benedict avoided it inwardly by divine help; and by his zeal rescued not only the lowliest, but also prelates of the Church. Armed with javelins of debate he often joined battle against the infamous doctrine.

2. There was at that time also a band of brothers already numerous and alight with ardor for eternal life. They vied indeed who of them might be humbler, who prompter in obedience, who more zealous in abstinence, who earlier at vigils, who slower to speak, who cheaper in dress, and who more fervent in charity. To certain of them revelations were even made.

CHAPTER NINE

There was a certain brother who was by no means disposed to human honor. When Father Benedict noticed that he was making his way apparently negligently, he concluded there was the same rudeness in his spirit. But caught up in an ecstasy the man saw a flock of doves, some gleaming with marvelous whiteness, some distinguished by an amazing variety of colors, some marked with a repulsive color on the head. Soon he realized what this meant and the names of each were spoken: negligence made some black, zeal made some gleam brightly. Returning to himself,[55] he related to Father Benedict what he had seen and warned him not to despise him. Searching the deeds of each, Benedict then discovered the minds of the brothers distraught, just as he learned from the ecstatic, and therefore restored them to suitable pattern by imposing a kindly emollient of reproof.

CHAPTER TEN

But the ancient foe tolerated with difficulty the unity and increase of the good flock. He tried to agitate the hearts of some to make the good founder an exile from his own sheepfold. By his craft he drove many away from the monastery and unsettled many others, though he could

54. See Introduction, p. 28.
55. Lk 15:17.

not dismay the mind prepared to tribulation. He nursed back to life latent forces that were broken and about to perish, by inciting them to take away horses and cattle both secretly and openly. But he who has set God before all things loses without grief what he possessed without love. Certainly no one ever saw Benedict upset over anything that was lost. He never sought to recover what was destroyed; he never looked for what was stolen. If a thief was caught, Benedict offered kindness and quietly released him so he would not be caught again.

CHAPTER ELEVEN

1. A certain fellow who stealthily removed the monastery's horses was captured and wounded by neighbors, and brought before Father Benedict. He furnished him expenses, summoned a physician, and sent him unharmed to the infirmary.

2. On another occasion, when the venerable father was making a journey in company with a brother, they met a man astride a horse stolen from the monastery. The brother stared inquiringly and recognized it as one that had been stolen. He immediately blurted out that it was the monastery's horse. But Benedict told him to keep quiet, 'One horse is often similar to another', he said. Aside he remonstrated with the brother, 'I, too, recognized it, but I think it is better to remain silent than to create a sense of embarrassment'.

CHAPTER TWELVE

1. Since almighty God, who created all things, on suitable occasions performs miracles through his servants, I will compress into a brief narrative some that he wrought through Benedict.

2. [56]Once upon a time a fire broke out in a house located near the basilica of the Blessed Virgin Mary. When the devouring flame licked at the dry thatch, the grieving brothers ran out together. They watched the house they had built with great labor being consumed by the leaping flames. They set about busying themselves with great effort to prevent the fire from spreading to the neighboring church, for the whole fury of the flame was tending in that direction. Father Benedict approached the spectacle. At once the brothers importuned him to help

56. First miracle story.

them with his prayers. Quickly complying with the brothers' urgency, he threw himself with tears before the altar of the Blessed Virgin Mary, Bearer of God. While he was praying, the fury of the fire suddenly turned with the aid of divine mercy in another direction.[57]

CHAPTER THIRTEEN

[58]At the same time, too, there was a great flight of locusts that hid the sun's rays with its thickness.[59] They settled in massed attack on the vineyard that lay near the monastery to devastate it. The brothers were accustomed to receive their cups chiefly from it. The venerable man entered the basilica of the Blessed God-bearer and with tear-drenched face and voice implored divine aid. After a little while the locusts became restless and left.

CHAPTER FOURTEEN

[60]By another chance fire attacked a neighboring mountain, licking at the dry straw, the branches, and the earth parched by the sun's heat. Moved by its own impetus, it threatened ruin to the vineyard and monastery. All the brothers ran out to extinguish it, and with them went the venerable Father Benedict. Suddenly the fire abandoned the path it had begun and quickly subsided on right and left. Except for Benedict's prayers, I think it must be supposed that conflagration would have prevailed.

CHAPTER FIFTEEN

[61]A certain brother was enjoined to guard the cattle. As he left the monastery to go to his duty, he sought the blessing of Father Benedict.

---

57. Precisely the same story is told of Alcuin, *Vita Alcuini,* 19, and in similar words. For the same kind of story, see Sulpicius, *Saint Martin,* 14 (Hoare, *Western Fathers,* 28).

58. Second miracle.

59. *Gregory the Great,* 10 (Jones, *Saint's Lives,* 104), has a miraculous story about locusts. Compare this with the strange account of a plague of locusts by Saint Augustine; see Allen Cabaniss, 'Two Notes on Augustine, Charlemagne, and Romance', *Augustinian Studies* 5 (1974) 77.

60. Third miracle.

61. Fourth miracle.

'May the Lord protect you', said the latter as he bestowed the sign of the cross. When the brother reached the pasture, he encountered two bandits. Approaching without any suspicion, he was halted by them. They seized the reins of the horse on which he was sitting. After peering at him a long time, they let him go without a word—and he left in a hurry. When he told the father, the latter remarked, 'God's blessing preserved you unharmed'.

CHAPTER SIXTEEN

What one has personally seen should not be passed over in silence. A certain brother was made prior. Falling into pride, he was deposed from his office. At length he became so spiteful that he decided to leave the monastery and practise robbery. So it was that he decided to steal a horse surreptitiously from the very monastery. When he tried to do so, Benedict commanded him to be driven away with his feet tied under the horse. But he began to bawl and swear that he would never depart from the monastery. Because of his folly, Benedict gave order to beat him lightly with switches. Thereafter he remained in the monastery, living properly and piously, as if the malign foe had been smitten in him.

CHAPTER SEVENTEEN

1. What is said thus far concerning the life of so great a father may be enough, as, by the light of divine clemency, he abandoned the world and removed to the regions of Gothia to erect by new endeavor a monastery. Now by Christ's aid let us unfold with clarity how by Charles's command he constructed another monastery in the same place.

2. In the year 782, the fourteenth of [the reign of] King Charles the Great, Benedict, with dukes and counts aiding him, undertook to construct another large church in honor of our Lord and Saviour, but differently. He covered the houses no longer with thatch but with tiles and he adorned the cloisters with as many marble columns as possible, which he placed in the porches. The place was furnished with such holiness that anyone who arrived seeking in faith would not doubt in his heart, but believe[62] that what he might need would come to pass.

62. James 1:6.

3. Because it glistened with outstanding religious observance, we deem it appropriate to relate for future generations some things about the location of that place. The venerable Father Benedict decided upon pious reflection to consecrate the aforesaid church, not by the title of one of the saints, but in the name of the Holy Trinity. For it to be more clearly recognized, he determined that three small altars should be placed near the main altar so that by them the persons of the Trinity might be figuratively indicated. A marvelous arrangement it is: by the three altars the undivided Trinity is shown forth and by the single altar the true Godhead in essence is shown forth. The great altar is one solid surface on the front, but inwardly concave. In figure it suggests what Moses built in the desert. It has a little door behind where on ferial day chests containing various relics of the fathers are enclosed. Enough said about the altar.

4. We now pass briefly to the furnishing of the building, in what order or number it is arranged. All the vessels that are kept in the building are consecrated to the number seven. For instance, there are seven candelabra curiously wrought by the craftsman's art. From the arms project branches, little spheres, with lilies, reeds, and bowls after the manner of a nut tree, made like that which Bezaleel contrived with his wonderful skill.[63] In front of the altar hang seven lamps, marvelous and very beautiful, wrought with incredible effort, lighted in the manner of Solomon by well-trained persons eager to tend them.[64]

5. In the same way other lamps of silver hang in the choir in the form of a crown, with containers inserted in circles. It is customary on special feasts to fill them with oil and light them. When they were lighted the whole church was aglow at night as if it were day. Lastly three further altars were dedicated in the basilica: one in honor Saint Michael the archangel; another in veneration of the blessed Apostles Peter and Paul; and a third in honor of gentle Stephen the protomartyr.

6. In the church of Blessed Mary, Bearer of God, which was the first established, there are altars of Saint Martin and also blessed Benedict. But the one which is built in the cemetery is distinguished by being consecrated in honor of Saint John the Baptizer, than whom among those born of women none greater has arisen, as the divine oracles

---

63. Ex 37:17–22; 36:1.
64. 2 Chr 8:14 and Ex 30:7.

testify.[65] To ponder with what profound humility and reverence this place was held in awe by them is appropriate, this place protected by so many princes. The Lord Christ is indeed the Prince of all princes, the King of kings and Lord of lords. Blessed Mary, the Bearer of God, is believed to be the queen of all virgins. Michael is set over all angels. Peter and Paul are chiefs of the apostles. Stephen the protomartyr holds first place in the choir of witnesses. Martin shines as the jewel of prelates. Benedict is the father of all monks. By the seven altars, by the seven candelabra, and by the seven lamps, the sevenfold grace of the Holy Spirit is understood.[66]

CHAPTER EIGHTEEN

1. Let anyone who seeks to read or listen to this biography, realize that Aniane is the head of all monasteries, not only of those erected in the regions of Gothia, but also of those erected in other areas at that time or afterwards according to its example and enriched with the treasures of Benedict, as this document will hereinafter relate. He gave his heart to studying the Rule of blessed Benedict. To be able fully to understand it, he visited various monasteries and inquired of experienced persons what he did not know. He assembled the rules of all the holy [monks] insofar as he could locate them. He became acquainted with a useful standard and wholesome customs for monasteries which he transmitted to his own monks to be observed. He established cantors, taught lectors, secured grammarians and experts in scriptural knowledge—of them some later became bishops.[67] He collected a multitude of books, assembled costly vestments, large silver chalices, and silver offertory vessels.

2. Whatever he observed to be needful for Divine Office he energetically obtained. He became known to everyone and the report of his holiness reached the ears of the emperor. Later he went to most glorious Emperor Charles for the benefit of the monastery. Moved by pious consideration, Charles granted possesion of the monastery to Benedict by charter, so that after the emperor's death the witnesses

65. Mt 11:1 *Gregory the Great*, 4 (Jones, *Saints' Lives*, 99), cites the same passage of Scripture.

66. Is 11:2f.

67. Sulpicius, *Saint Martin*, 10 (Hoare, *Western Fathers*, 25): many of his students become bishops.

would not permit any disruptions by his family. From Charles Benedict
soon received an 'immunity' containing the following:

3. 'In the name of the holy and undivided Trinity, Charles, by
God's grace king of the Franks and Lombards and patrician of
the Romans.[68] We believe that fortification of our realm will
reach its greatest peak if, with well-wishing devotion, we con-
cede suitable locations as benefices for churches. With the
Lord's protection we decree they are to endure without varia-
tions. Be it therefore known to all bishops, abbots, counts,
viscounts, vicars, hundred-men, judges, and all the faithful,
present and future alike, how the venerable man, Abbot Benedict, came to our clemency from the monastery he himself
built up by new effort and by his own right from the ground
up in honor of our Lord and Saviour, Jesus Christ, of the holy
and ever-virgin Mary Bearer of God, and of other saints, in
the place called Aniane, in the countryside of Maguelonne,
near the fortress of Montcalm. With fullest purpose he assigned
to our hands the aforesaid monastery with all properties and
ornaments of the church, whether attached to it or adjacent,
and committed that holy place to be ruled by us under our
dominion and defense.

4. At his special petition, therefore, we have granted, for the
sake of eternal reward, a benefit to that holy place in this manner. In respect of churches, places, fields, or other properties of
that monastery, which it rightly has in modern times by our
gift and confirmation or that of other of the faithful, in whatever location, whatever has been assembled there for the sake
of divine love, whatever else the divine loving-kindness may
hereafter add by right to that holy place, whether by us or by
others, we command them to receive. Moreover we enjoin,
order, and anathematize that no count, no bishop, nor any
judicial power dare at any time ever to enter or presume to
force cases to be heard, taxes to be levied, habitations or provisions to be seized, sponsors to be taken away, persons of that
monastery, free or servants, who live on its lands to be removed,

68. Mühlbacher, *Regesta Imperii* (Innsbruck, Wagner'sche Universitäts-
Buchhandlung, 1877–.) No. 318, dated 27 July 792.

any cancelled sales or unlawful pretexts to be sought, or any property to be questioned.

5. The abbot himself, his successors, and the monks, present or future, may rule the aforesaid place for the sake of God's name under complete immunity without disturbance or opposition by anyone whatever; nor may they ever dare for any reason to divert its property to anyone. We desire to confirm that holy place is under our defense and governance. We therefore declare and command that neither you nor your juniors or successors, or anyone with judicial power shall ever, at any time, dare to make disturbances or exactions in the churches, places, fields, or other possessions of the monastery aforesaid or indeed make changes in any of the matters written above; but may what we, for the sake of the Lord's name and of eternal reward, have granted to the aforementioned monastery, increase and grow to time out of mind.

6. Whenever, at the divine summons, the venerable Abbot Benedict mentioned above or his successors depart this life to the Lord, that holy congregation wishes to choose an abbot from the monastery described above or from whatever place, an abbot of similar kind or better, one faithful to us in all matters, one able to govern that holy congregation according to Saint Benedict's Rule, they have permission to do so by this our authority and indulgence. Wherever they and their monks may wish to be regulated or by whatever prelate, they have authority by our precept and consent, so long as those servants of God belonging to God's household in that place may be pleased to pray constantly for the Lord's mercy upon us, upon our wife and children; and for the stability of the entire realm committed and spared to us by God.

CHAPTER NINETEEN

1. The most glorious King Charles conferred these thing by precept upon the venerable man Benedict,[69] but the latter also received from him from all directions through the imperial charter useful cattle and lands suitable for farming. Dowered by the emperor with great honor—

69. *Ibid.*, No. 349, June 799.

that is, almost forty pounds of silver—he returned in peace to his monastery as quickly as possible. As soon as he reached his native land, he dispatched the silver he bore, divided for the sake of blessing, to the several monasteries. In our times he had this singular gift beyond all others, namely, a kindly and responsible respect for everyone and a concern for all the monasteries whether near at hand or at a distance. He visited them frequently and imbued them with the regulations of holy living.

2. Of those materials conferred on him by the faithful, he passed them on according to the number of inhabitants and according to their ability, more to those in greater want, less to those requiring little. For he knew monasteries of both kinds and he remembered their names. But because he could not distribute mantles to each one, he sent them divided and made into crosses. Of all the monasteries, whether situated in Provence or in Gothia and the province of Gascony[70], he was like a nurse cherishing and aiding. He was beloved by all as father, venerated as master, and revered as teacher.

3. A portion for the poor was set aside with greatest energy and he did not allow widows' shares to be expended for other purposes. He knew of course the names of all the nuns and widows located round-about. Ransom was joyfully provided for captives. No one departing left him without a gift and as far as possible everything was done for everyone. For that reason each person voluntarily brought provisions to him to be laid up for distribution to the poor, needy, widows, captives, and monks. From some people he might receive as much as four or five thousand *solidi* in vessels to be apportioned among those in want.

4. Benedict had great concern not only to refresh his own people with the food of preaching, but also to nourish with heavenly bread whomever he happened to encounter. That they might not lose the salutary food through forgetfulness, he was accustomed to impress upon them to cling tenaciously to it in their heart. 'Be of chaste body and humble heart,' he said, 'because proud chastity and vain humility are not acceptable to God'. On some he was in the habit of stressing this: 'If most precepts are impossible for you to remember, keep at least this short one. *Turn away from evil and do good*'.[71] That statement was so

70. *Novempalitana.*
71. Ps 37 [36]:27.

habitual to him that near the time of his death, when he had assembled statements from all the fathers, he proposed to produce one book about it alone. At every hour, whether at Nocturns,[72] in chapter, or in refectory, he provided the food of life for all those subject to him.

CHAPTER TWENTY

While we have tried to describe his good will, a number of his virtues stand out in plain view. We will, therefore, detail a small section of them suitable for men who do not know about them, but desire the information. Everyone attached to his 'family' knows this—that he surpassed all others in charity. Never did he do anything for himself but rather what he deemed beneficial to others. If he did otherwise, he quickly made reparation. Out of love of charity and in order to secure the salvation of many, he visited the cells of others and explained the obscurities of the holy Rule. Filled with charity, he spent days in Arles with many bishops, abbots, and monks,[73] explaining the mysteries of the canons and expounding the homilies of the blessed Pope Gregory to the ignorant. What is more, filled with charity he nurtured within his own monastery clergy and monks from different localities. Appointing a teacher for them, he saturated them with sacred interpretations. In charity he sent gifts to those who did injury to him. But we should not belabor describing what everyone better saw and many in his service experienced.

CHAPTER TWENTY-ONE

1. From the rigor of his first way of life, Benedict little by little turned away[74] for he had undertaken an impossible task, yet the same will remained. He ploughed with ploughmen, accompanied diggers, reaped with reapers. Although that region was scorched by the sun's heat—a heat as though of fire from a furnace, burning rather than heating—he rarely allowed his men, even when suffering from excessive heat, a cup of water before the hour of refreshment. Worn with labor, scorched by the heat, they desired cold water rather than wine. But no one grumbled

---

72. The office of Vigils.
73. A council was convened in Arles in May 813 by the emperor.
74. *declinarat*: the word probably implies disapproval.

against him, because he endured the same. That fact brought them no little solace, for he acted more leniently toward them when he observed himself burning with thirst. Nor did any of those working dare to make noise by chatting; instead, their hands were occupied with work and their tongues with psalmody. The mouths of those going to and returning from work were intent on divine meditations.

2. Often we saw him even strike the hands of those who attempted to treat him more humanely in drink and food. We also observed him measuring the dish set before him. And those who were in charge of the cellar related that while others were drinking wine, he usually drank water—except on the Sabbath and the Lord's Day.[75] We often separated any fat from his food and special care was taken lest even a small particle of common cheese be found in it. From the day of his conversion to the end of his life he chose not to eat the flesh of four-footed animals.[76] If any weakness overtook him, he took a broth made from a chicken.

3. For many years in his earlier day he avoided fat, yet as often as there was opportunity he provided for others what he denied himself. So great was his solicitude that if a tiny grain of vegetable, a small fragment of chicken, or cabbage leaves were overlooked by anyone, a suitable sentence of excommunication[77] was meted out for him whose fault it was proven to be. If anyone drew water for him for washing and poured more than was necessary—as did happen—he had to acknowledge that he had sinned by not walking the road of discretion.

4. Benedict possessed an unusual gift: as soon as anyone with disturbed thoughts in his mind approached him, the tumultuous crowd of thoughts dissipated at his wholesome counsel. Often indeed when a person was bombarded by defiled thoughts (so I learned from a true brother), he would say to himself, 'I will go and lay you before Lord Benedict'. At that very moment the troublesome confusion left him. If anyone was hindered by severer faults, he received soothing consolation when he opened his heart to Benedict. If someone was tormented by the disease of melancholy, after visiting Benedict he soon departed happy.[78]

75. See Introduction, p. 46.
76. RB 39.11.
77. RB 24.3. A disciplinary measure.
78. Felix, *Saint Guthlac*, 45 (Jones, *Saints' Lives*, 150), left no one without consolation even though melancholy.

CHAPTER TWENTY-TWO

The throng of monks engaged in God's service so increased that there were more than three hundred. Because of the extraordinary company, Benedict ordered a bigger house be built, one able to hold a thousand or more men. It was a hundred cubits in length and twenty in width. And because other places could not hold them, he constructed cells at suitable locations at which he placed brothers with teachers to direct them.

CHAPTER TWENTY-THREE

[79]About that time a downpour occurred while the brothers and their teacher were resting. Suddenly the streaming water rushed in at both doors and threatened to fill the house where they were resting. The frightened brothers got up in a hurry. A latrine had been built with great effort over running water which began to rise and threaten to overturn it. The rivulets below began to surge with a roar and leaped up in waves at that moment to ruin the structure. Although it was nearly midnight the monks ran to the church. There the father himself had already arrived. He seized the bell rope and ordered them to sing Lauds, to implore the suffrages of the saints, and to entreat God's mercy with tears. After many prayers they went out to see whether the building was overthrown. As the venerable man was going, the night was so dark and gloomy that he ran into a bramble bush and hurt his legs, and over-whelmed with distress, he tearfully begged God that the flood would abate. When they reached the place, the water was found to have sub-sided by a whole foot. Relying on God's help they returned to their companions in the church. When having related God's kindness, they blessed God together.

CHAPTER TWENTY-FOUR

1. In the meantime some bishops, hearing reports of Benedict's sanctity and the holy reputation of his flock, began insistently to request some monks from him to serve as examples. Among them Leidrad, bishop of Lyons, wanting to rebuild the monastery of Ile-Barbe, sought with insistence those who might display for him the beginning of the good

79. Fifth miracle.

life. Benedict thereupon selected some twenty students from his flock, set a director over them, and instructed them to take up residence in the region of Burgundy. With the Lord's assistance there has now been assembled in that area a large band of monks, thriving and flourishing in holy religion.

2. Theodulf, bishop of Orléans,[80] desirous of erecting the monastery of Saint Maximin, also requested of the aforesaid holy man some experts in the discipline of the Rule. The latter quickly gave assent and dispatched to him twice ten monks[81] with a teacher set over them. Since they continually vied in holy zeal, they added to themselves no small band of monks.

3. [82]I will relate what occurred there when the venerable father approached them for a visit. Awaiting his arrival, they devoted their energy to procuring an abundant supply of fish and foods, not only out of love for him, but also for all the brothers. There was a meeting of the brothers; fishermen were dispatched; markets were searched. But so much difficulty was involved that nothing could be found for purchase; the fish would not bite. They were filled with great sorrow at this barren result. In the meanwhile the master arrived. They received him joyously and he, rejoicing in their progress, greeted them in return. The brothers concealed their chagrin under cheerful countenances.

4. Later it happened that a certain brother was diligently pursuing his effort alongside the river Loire. Suddenly he spied a large fish, one they call a salmon, swimming near the bank. With no hesitation, the brother jumped in to catch it and bring it to the others. There was joy over this, but there was even more wonderment, for they all professed that this came about owing to the merits of venerable Benedict. Unless I am in error, I learned this from a faithful brother.

5. Alcuin, of the nation of Angles, a deacon in rank,[83] outstanding in wisdom, venerable by merit of holiness, governing the monastery of the blessed confessor Martin (who had been bishop of Tours), was held worthy of full honor at the court of glorious Emperor Charles. When Alcuin heard about and experienced the holiness of the man of God,

---

80. See introduction, p. 38.
81. Cf. RB 21:1-2.
82. Sixth miracle.
83. *ordine levites*: a levite in rank.

he linked himself to him in inviolable charity. From his letters addressed to Benedict, a booklet has been compiled.[84] Once gifts had been offered, Alcuin resolutely demanded that some monks be given to him. The venerable father at once complied and Alcuin dispatched horses to fetch them. He situated them in a monastery named Cormery, which he had erected. There were, I think, twenty with a teacher set over them. By the good example of their way of life a great multitude of monks was assembled.

CHAPTER TWENTY-FIVE

1. I do not think it amiss if miracles done by divine grace at this time are inserted in this treatise.

2. [85]A certain brother was sent to carry from one cell to another a consecrated container in which relics of Saint Denis and other saints had been put. With him he took along also some puppies, but returning after several days he heedlessly strove to bring back the consecrated container without having washed his clothing. He embarked hurriedly in a boat—for his cell was situated between a lake and the sea. As soon as he reached land, he mounted a horse, settling the puppies first and then picking up the container to transport it. But divine punishment overthrew him. At that very moment the horse reared in a circular motion until the brother tumbled to the ground. The container slipped from his hands, though it was later recovered unharmed. The horse died on the spot, and the brother who had fallen was taken away unconscious. He remained that way a long time, but ultimately regained his health.

3. When the brothers learned what had happened, they sent another brother back to look for the relics. Being a priest, he took along a cross in which some of the Lord's wood was embedded. As he entered the lake his small boat was shaken by a mighty wind. But as soon as he held up to the swelling waves the cross which he wore about his neck, the winds subsided.[86] While he was resting in his cell, he had seen in a dream a man of dazzling brightness who addressed him thus: 'Unless you take with you the Lord's wood, you will never leave here at the time you

84. Only the letters cited in introduction, pp. 37–38, have been preserved.

85. Seventh miracle.

86. Constantius, *Saint Germanus*, 12 (Hoare, *Western Fathers*, 296f.), worked the same kind of miracle.

want'. And so he was warned to carry the relics on foot. But he did not obey and, when he recovered and returned them, he was stricken with severe illness. Afterwards, in the church from which the relics were removed there hung a lamp in the reservoir of which there was very little oil. But on the next day they were found to be full. That happened three times. I learned this story from the brother who had fallen ill.

CHAPTER TWENTY-SIX [87]

In the mountains where the brothers were living, they erected a small oratory for prayer while they had the task of pasturing the sheep. After the brothers departed from that place, some women entered it. Jeering at the tiny dwellings of the monks, they said to one another, 'You take the abbot's position and stand in his place'. And as they stood in the place of prayer, as though praying, and took turns kneeling down, they had difficulty in rising. Those dwellings in which the monks lived only during summer time remained vacant, yet suitable punishment overtook the women at once. They began to be wracked with jerks and twists.[88] They were not rescued from the pain until their husbands followed the monks as they went down the mountain with the sheep and begged them to offer prayers for the brash women. As the brothers prayed, the women were instantly restored to health.

CHAPTER TWENTY-SEVEN [89]

1. A demon-possessed man from some place came to the monastery, led by his parents. He was placed in the basilica of the blessed and ever-virgin Mary, Bearer of God. When the brothers poured out prayers for him at vigils, his health returned and he left in peace.

2. A woman filled with an unclean spirit came to the monastery. The brothers guarded her with vigils and prayers in the oratory of Saint John the baptizer, which is located at the cemetery. With God's help she, too, left in safe condition.

---

87. Eighth miracle.

88. Sulpicius, *Saint Martin*, 12 (Hoare, *Western Fathers*, 26), turning around in ridiculous whirligigs; cf. the folk story of the mad dancers of Kolbeck.

89. Ninth and tenth miracles.

CHAPTER TWENTY-EIGHT [90]

1. If, to the oratory dedicated in honor of Saint Saturninus the martyr, where the venerable man Benedict first began to dwell, anyone with fever went and slept a little while, he would return in sound condition to his own estates—if he did not waver in faith.

2. Let it suffice to have said these few things about miracles done in our times. With God's aid let us return to the sequence we began.[91]

CHAPTER TWENTY-NINE

The most glorious Louis, then king of Aquitaine but now by God's provident grace emperor Augustus of the whole church in Europe,[92] discovered Benedict's way of holiness, loved him beyond measure, and freely obeyed his counsel. The emperor set him over all the monasteries in his realm[93] to exhibit to all a wholesome standard. For there were certain monasteries observing canonical institutes, but unaware of the precepts of the Rule. Obeying Louis's commands, Benedict traveled around to each of the monasteries, not once or twice only, but many times, showing them the admonitions of the Rule and discussing it with them chapter by chapter, confirming what was known, revealing what was unknown. By God's foresight it therefore came to pass that almost all the monasteries located in Aquitaine accepted the plan of the Rule.

2. But he who ever hates good deeds, the opponent of innocence and enemy of peace, deemed it unfair if Benedict persisted a long time in the pious king's friendship, not hesitating to inflict damage if their love remained undivided. And because he had lost the glory of his own nature by pride, he is on guard with all his prowess against any human being introduced into those good things that he lost. He laments that a human should be recovered by God's mercy. It is no wonder that the ancient foe is tortured by the uprightness of pious persons and that he persecutes those whom he observes to be invincible in their progress.

90. Eleventh miracle.

91. *Gregory the Great*, 18 (Hoare, *Western Fathers*, 107), 'But, to return to the subject'.

92. Notice the unusual title.

93. Cf. 36.1 below.

Nonetheless there are many who emulate Satan's wicked works. Although it is to be deeply lamented, many burn with alien practices; they are armed with hatred against those who choose not to follow their example.

3. When the aforesaid deeds were recognized as outstanding and meritorious to God, Satan, overwhelmed by their number, armed with weapons of envy, set forth to fight them with evil. First he fired the minds of the clergy to belittle them. Then he invaded the hearts of knights of the royal court and subverted the minds of certain counts. Equally inflamed with the tinder of envy—not secretly but openly vomiting the venom of a pestilent mind—they all raised a public outcry that he who always prayed for their souls was a 'wandering monk',[94] greedy for property, an invader of other people's estates. Their mad fury exploded to such enormity that they tried to provoke the most serene Emperor Charles against Benedict.

4. But the man of God, his conscience quite secure, was neither dismayed by the belittlement nor frightened by false accusations. He therefore approached the palace about the matter. Along the way a few tried to stop him, claiming that if he appeared in the emperor's presence he would not be allowed to return to his homeland, because imperial anger was aroused against him. He went in, however, without trepidation, relying on God's pity and putting his hope in Him for love of whom he strove without reluctance. If he should be sentenced to undergo pain of exile, so be it. It would make his mind freer to serve God. If he should be removed from office, and no longer superior, he explained that with deep yearning he had long desired that boon. But when he appeared in the emperor's presence heavenly loving-kindness inclined Charles's mind to such great peace that, as soon as he saw Benedict, he embraced him and with his own hand extended a cup to him. And he, whom envious men had claimed would be an exile from his own soil, returned to it with great honor. And so, with divine mercy overriding, those who tried to defame him actually praised him[95] and showed him, whom they sought to render odious by lies, revered not only by the least, but also by the greatest.

94. *circillionem.*
95. Sulpicius, *Saint Martin*, 9 (Hoare, *Western Fathers*, 23).

CHAPTER THIRTY [96]

1. Count William, who was more outstanding at the emperor's court than all others, clung to blessed Benedict with such fondness that he scorned the dignities of the world and chose him as his leader in that way of salvation by which he might attain to Christ.[97] Having at length received permission to be converted [to monastic life], he bestowed on the venerable man vast amounts of gold, silver, and costly vestments. William endured no delay in allowing his hair to be shorn. On the birthday of the Apostles Peter and Paul,[98] he laid aside clothes woven of gold and put on the habit of Christ-followers, rejoicing that he was so quickly added to the number of heaven-dwellers.[99]

2. There was a valley about four miles away from blessed Benedict's monastery. It was called Gellone. There the aforesaid count, hitherto so well placed in the world's dignity, gave order to construct a cell wherein he committed himself to serve Christ for the duration of his life. Although born of noble origin, he was zealous to make himself Christ's by embracing a nobler poverty. For Christ he rejected the highest honor he had inherited.

3. I think it worthwhile to relate—for those who do not know—some of the deeds of his devout manner of life. In the aforesaid cell the venerable Father Benedict had already placed his monks. Imbued with their example, within a few days William excelled in virtues those by whom he was taught. With the aid of his sons[100] whom he had set over his counties and neighboring counts, he quickly brought to completion the fabric of the monastery he had begun. That place was so remote that anyone dwelling here could not wish for solitude. On all sides it was surrounded by cloud-covered mountains. No one had access to it but one whom a willing spirit drew there for the sake of prayer. It was bathed in such pleasantness that one could desire no other place if he decided to serve God. Vineyards were there which the aforesaid man ordered planted, an abundance of gardens, a valley packed with different kinds of trees. He acquired a great many possessions.

96. On Chapter Thirty, an interpolation on William of Gellone, see the Introduction, pp. 45–52.

97. Phil 3:8.

98. 29 June.

99. *Christicolarum . . . coelicolarum.*

100. His sons were Bernard and Gaucelm.

4. At his request, the most serene King Louis expanded it with a spacious boundary, granting from his own treasure funds to work the areas. The king gave a great many sacred vestments, furnished silver and gold chalices and vessels for the offertory, brought along a great many books, draped the altars with gold and silver. Having entered into this cell William dedicated himself wholly to Christ, abandoning all trace of worldly ostentation.[101] He was of such profound humility that seldom if ever could a monk whom he happened to meet bow low enough not to be surpassed by him in humbleness. We often saw him mount his donkey to carry flagons of wine to the barn, himself seated thereon bearing a chalice over his shoulders on his back, visiting the brothers of our monastery at harvest time to slake their thirst. At vigils he was so wakeful that he surpassed everyone. At the mill he worked with his own hands unless another occupation hindered or illness impeded him. He took his turn in the kitchen. In dress he wore the standard vesture of deepest humility. He was a lover of fasting, constant in prayer, unwearying in compunction. Scarcely ever did he receive the body of Christ without streams of tears falling to earth. He avidly sought harshness of bed, but because of his poor health Father Benedict had a coverlet spread beneath him although he did not want it.

5. Some say that for love of Christ William often had himself flogged with whips, but no one other than the person who was present was aware of that practice. Often during the middle of the night and shivering with the icy cold and clad with one thin cloak, he remained in the oratory that he had erected in honor of Saint Michael he was—known only to God—absorbed in prayer. For a few years he was filled with these and other virtues. Then he realized that the day of death was threatening him. He ordered it to be made known in writing to almost all the monasteries in Lord Charles' realm when he had departed from this world. In this manner, bearing a supply of virtues, he left the world when Christ summoned him. For those desirous of knowing, this is enough said. Let us again return to the work we undertook.[102]

101. See introduction, p. 50 and note.
102. Cf. 28.2 above and note 88 above.

CHAPTER THIRTY-ONE

The most pious King Louis, knowing how usual it is for lovers of this world to resent the advancement of righteous persons, associated himself more closely in loving esteem with Benedict as the venerable abbot was ridiculed more and more by madmen. The queen,[103] too, cherished him with pious attachment. Because she had come to know he was just man, she willingly paid attention to him and very often bestowed gifts on him. When the crowd of students grew and the place where Benedict dwelt was unfruitful, the ground almost barren, and scorched with the sun's heat, Louis gave him the monastery situated in the Auvergne which Saint Menelaus, scion of royal origin, had founded and where his body lay. Thither Benedict directed twelve monks, setting over them as abbot a man of highest respect named Andoar, a man well-proven and worn by many toils, who had been with him from the earliest day of his conversion. As they labored and strove with holy zeal, seventy or more joined them to practice monastic life as fully as possible.

2. On one occasion the eminent Abbot Benedict went to that monastery to visit the brothers. While the abbot and brothers were awaiting his arrival at a particular place, it happened that Benedict entered that cell of the monastery where the church in honor of our God and Saviour is located. The brothers had indeed at first taken up residence there, but because it was a narrow place the most serene king had transferred them to the monastery already mentioned above. The brothers who were left behind to care for the cell were delighted when they saw the abbot approaching with some of his monks. They were embarrassed, however, because they were very poor. But where charity is, even a little is enough, so he who presided over the brothers ordered one of them to fetch wine. He replied that there was no wine in the vessel. The other brothers had left with them only two small vessels in which there was just enough wine with which they could chant Mass or sip a single serving on Sundays.

3.[104] The master of that cell was downcast when he heard there was no wine in the vessel, but he said confidently. 'Go and bring it to us. Those who are going ahead to meet him should drink out of respect

103. The queen may have been Irmingard, Louis' first wife, or else Judith, his second, or both.

104. The twelfth miracle.

for the father. It will not fail them.'The brother went and as he turned
the spigot wine came out! When he had first tried to get some and did
not succeed, he had returned. Now he told them what was happening.
Those who were present glorified God and declared that it was accomplished by the merits of Lord Benedict. They drank, therefore, at
will and took some with them to refresh the travelers. Lord Benedict
arrived with his monks and accepted what was needful and took some
of it with him on his journey. Thereafter the vessel again ceased to yield
wine. I learned this from those very brothers who told me what they
saw; some of these witnesses still living.[105]

CHAPTER THIRTY-TWO[106]

At another time Benedict went back to the same monastery. When,
after a long sermon and holy conversation,[107] he was getting ready to
depart, he offered the kiss of peace to the brothers. A certain brother
among them approached for the kiss. When the man of God saw him
he stopped at once and for a moment refused the kiss of peace. Then,
after a suitable rebuke at which we wondered, he kissed the brother.
Another brother then presented himself. Benedict did the same to him.
Finally, after a last farewell, he left the brothers. On the morning after
he went away it was discovered that those two brothers had been in-
tending to run away. Then we understood why the venerable *abba*[108],
under the Holy Spirit's revelation, had been slow to embrace them.
Even if he did not openly betray their perverse intention, he nevertheless chided their disturbed consciences with salutary words.

CHAPTER THIRTY-THREE

The most glorious king gave Benedict yet another monastery, to which,
I believe, he sent twenty monks and an abbot. That monastery was situ-
ated in the region of Poitiers and dedicated in honor of Saint Savinus.
While the brothers placed there kept watch and sweated away diligently

105. 1 Cor 15:6.
106. The thirteenth miracle.
107. Acts 20:11.
108. Here and at the other places where it appears in Latin (35.2; 37.2), I have
preserved the Aramaic *abba*.

in holy undertakings, no small band of monks were joined to them. Again Louis conferred on him another monastery, located in the region of Bourges. There Benedict settled about forty monks and an abbot. Since that place was founded as an entirely new effort, he provided assistance and gave them books and vestments. While they were flourishing in the habit of holy religion, displaying a standard of holy monastic observance and preserving unity of spirit in the bond of peace,[109] they were gathering into Christ's sheepfold a very large flock of monks.

CHAPTER THIRTY-FOUR

An illustrious nobleman, Wulfar by name, kinsman of Count William, gave them by charter a place to erect a monastery in the confines of Albi. Thither Benedict sent about twelve monks with an abbot ordained for them. Because they had enough to do to complete by new effort the fabric of the monastery they had undertaken, he also gave them a great many books, provided them sacred vestments, and managed a silver chalice, offertory vessels, a cross, and everything he perceived would be necessary for them. As they struggled both in the construction of material buildings and in the edification of souls by the regulations of the holy Rule, they acquired a large congregation of religious brothers in the service of Christ God.

CHAPTER THIRTY-FIVE

1. After the death of most serene Emperor Charles and after his son, King Louis of Aquitaine, assumed care of the empire, he ordered Benedict into the region of Frankland. Louis designated Marmoutier in Alsace, where Benedict had located many followers of his lifestyle from the monastery of Aniane. And because the aforesaid place was at such a distance from the palace that Benedict could not meet at an opportune time when he was summoned, and because he was required by the emperor for many matters, it pleased Louis to provide him a convenient place not far from the palace where he could live with a few monks. So it was an abbot was set over the brothers at Marmoutier, while Benedict himself went with several in obedience to the emperor's will.

109. Eph 4:3.

2. There was a neighboring valley which is, I think, not more than six miles from the palace. It was pleasing in the eyes of the man of God. There the emperor ordered the construction, with amazing effort, of a monastery called Inde, the name of the valley itself and derived from the little river.[110] The emperor was present for the dedication of the church and he endowed it abundantly from his own treasures. He gave it immunity and decreed in a written document[111] that thirty monks should dwell there in the service of Christ God. To complete the number, the venerable *abba* commanded brothers selected from noted monasteries to come, whom he might instruct by his example to be lessons of salvation to others, until others from that province, animated by divine grace, having abandoned secular pomp, and seeking knightly service for the eternal King,[112] might in time be chosen for the order.

3. After that the man of God began to wear away the palace floors and, for the profit of many, to endure troubles he had once set aside. All who suffered from injuries of others or who sought imperial opinions came to him. He received them with gladness and embraced them. At an opportune moment he brought their complaints set down in documents to the emperor. The most serene emperor, plucking at his kerchief or sleeves,[113] received them, read them as he obtained them, and after becoming acquainted with them decided as usefully as he knew how. But sometimes he put them away and forgot them.[114] Yet the emperor willingly listened to complaints of this kind and for that reason ordered Benedict to be at the palace as unremittingly as possible.

4. There were very many who consulted the abbot about the direction of the realm, about the disposition of provinces, and about their own advantage. No one, in fact, was as compassionate on the wretchedness of the afflicted, no one revealed to the emperor the needs of monks as did he. He was an advocate of the wretched, but a father of monks; a comforter of the poor, but a teacher of monks. He provided the food of life to the rich, but he inculcated the discipline of the Rule in the

110. *Chronicon Moissiacense*, 814 (SS 1:311), and Ermoldus Nigellus, *In honorem Hludowici*, 2:555f.

111. No longer extant.

112. Note the use of military terminology for monastic service.

113. An interesting sidelight on Louis's nervousness.

114. Also on his forgetfulness.

minds of monks. Although he took thought for the advantage of all persons, he intervened zealously in the needs of monks.

CHAPTER THIRTY-SIX

1. The emperor therefore set Benedict over all monasteries in his realm,[115] that as he had instructed Aquitaine and Gothia in the standard of salvation, so also might he imbue Frankland by his salutary example. Many monasteries had once been established according to the Rule but little by little firmness had grown lax and regular order had almost perished. That there might be one wholesome usage for all monasteries, as there was one profession by all, the emperor ordered the fathers of monasteries to assemble with as many monks as possible. They were in session for very many days.[116] Once they all had come together, Benedict elucidated obscure points to all as he discussed the entire Rule; he made clear doubtful points; he swept away old errors; he confirmed useful customs and arrangements. The directives of the Rule and questionable points he explained with keen result, as well as customs the Rule did not mention. Everyone gave assent. On all this Benedict then prepared for the emperor a chapter by chapter decree[117] for confirmation to enjoin these observances in all monasteries of his realm. We refer the inquiring reader to that document.[118]

2. The emperor immediately gave his assent and appointed inspectors for each monastery to oversee whether those things that were enjoined were observed and to transmit the wholesome standard to those unaware of it. By the aid of divine mercy the task was happily accomplished. All monasteries were returned to a degree of unity as if taught by one teacher in one place. Uniform measure in drink and food, in vigils and singing, was decreed to be observed by all. And because Benedict established observance of the Rule throughout other monasteries, he instructed his own at Inde so that monks going from other regions might not engage in the noisy conversation to which they were accustomed, but might

115. Cf. 29.1 above.
116. See introduction, pp. 28f and note.
117. Capitulary.
118. *Acta* of the General Synods of Aachen, ed. Kassius Hallinger, in *Corpus Consuetudinum Monasticarum* I (Siegburg 1963).

see the standard and discipline of the Rule portrayed in usage, walk, and dress of the monks at Inde.

CHAPTER THIRTY-SEVEN

1. Because of the indiscreet warmth of many, the unwarranted tepidness of some, and the obtuse sensibility of those with less capacity, Benedict established a boundary and gave to all an arrangement to be observed, restraining some from seeking superfluous exertions, commanding others to shake off sluggishness, admonishing still others to fulfill at least what they aspired to. He ordered many rules to be observed, but there are a great many matters demanded in daily practice about which the Rule is silent. Yet by them a monk's habit is adorned as if with jewels and without them it appears to be careless, monotonous, and disorganized.

2. For the sake of unity and concord or perhaps for the sake of honorable appearance or even out of consideration for human frailty, he commanded several things that are not inculcated in the Rule. On this account the venerable *abba* of holy memory ascertained what should be observed and ordered them fulfilled without delay or pretext of excuse. Those matters which for certain reasons should be remitted or changed, he did not consider but entrusted them to his students to be observed in some measure as he could differentiate according to possibility or according to place. Where any page of the Rule explains less than lucidly or remains altogether silent, he established and supplied with reason and aptness some matters on which, with divine help, I will touch briefly as follows.

CHAPTER THIRTY-EIGHT

1. First, how the bell was to be rung for the night hours. Benedict ordered that a small bell in the brothers' dormitory be tapped, so that the gathering of monks deep in prayer might first occupy their own places and then later,[119] when the doors of the church were opened, entry might be permitted to guests. Rising quickly, as the Rule orders, the brothers should sprinkle themselves with holy water and hasten humbly and reverently to all the altars, then go to their places so that

---

119. Ardo numbers the first and third bells, but not the second.

when the third bell is rung they may stand without delay, with ears attuned, awaiting the priest designated to begin the office.

2. During this interval no one allowed to enter was permitted to stand in corners of the church, but stationed in choir they were inaudibly to intone the prescribed psalms. He ordered them to sing psalms: five for all the faithful living throughout the whole world, then five for all the faithful departed, and five for those who were recently departed.[120] He decreed that the last five be sung comprehensively, for there was no reason regularly to mention specific deceased persons. When those last five psalms were completed, each was to prostrate himself in prayer, commending to God those in general for whom he sang: and only then begin to make petition for others. As one's body lies on the earth there should be no reluctance to supplicate the eternal King in specially prescribed psalms. One should not fear to bow his head at designated words along with others able to do so, since in this manner divine grace is suitably invoked and the fervor of compunction is aroused.

3. In summer time, when the office of Matins is over, Benedict ordered the monks to go outside the church if they were sleepy. Putting on their sandals and washing their faces, they could then return fully alert and, as before, go around the altars with reverence, sprinkle themselves with holy water, and then go to the places assigned to each to complete the daily office in an honorable manner, as well as those offices which are, according to Roman use, rendered with Psalm 118.[121] He ordered the bell to be rung a long time so they could assemble while it was ringing, but when it stopped the priest was to begin the Hour. When Prime was over, they were to disperse to assemble in chapter. When that was over, they could then go out to the work assigned to them either in silence or singing psalms. Those who remained at the monastery must not be occupied in idle stories[122] but two by two or even singly they were to sing psalms whether in kitchen, mill, or cellar. But he decreed that after Compline no one was to go outside freely or linger in the oratory;

4. but in winter time they should sing ten Psalms; in summer, five. Then, when the last bell is rung, all should walk together around all the

120. The gradual psalms 120–134 (Vulgate 119–133).
121. Ps 119 in the Hebrew Psalter.
122. *fabulis . . . ociosis*; cf. 41.1 below.

altars in the aforesaid manner, and thereafter go to sleep, each on his own bed. At those three times each day he commanded them to go around all the altars. At the first one they should say the Lord's Prayer and the Creed; at the others, the Lord's Prayer; or they should confess their lapses. At the day hours for prayer, each should go to his own place to pray. If, however, someone has a particular reason to pray alone, he should do so only by permission and only at whatever hour he was not otherwise occupied. Benedict established those three stations of prayer so that those who were sluggish, slow, or not in a mood to pray might at least do under compulsion what they did not want to do freely and not presume to abandon the appointed hours, while those who were aflame with extreme love might be restrained from indiscreetly seeking extra hours. Thus it came to pass that they were not worn away with excessive or indiscreet vigils during the course of one night and hence preoccupied at the hours when one should be intent on divine psalms, since one cannot discharge the divine requirement while sleepy.

5. The custom of many had in the past caused them also to dress differently. The cowls of some hung down to their ankles. The man of God man therefore instituted a uniform style to be worn by all monks: the length should not extend more than two cubits or reach to the knees. Out of necessity he conceded beyond what the Rule decrees, two woolen shirts, trousers, leather cloaks and coverings, and two capes. Whatever he observed as necessary to diminish evasion by any pretext, he conceded and allowed.

6. In a written statement to the emperor, Benedict gave his opinion on those matters which the Rule directs but which for good reason remained untried, as well as on those matters on which it was silent but which were usefully to be introduced. He directed his full desire toward observance of the Rule; it was his overriding endeavor that nothing might escape his knowledge. Consequently he interrogated minutely those whom he found to be experienced, whether living nearby or at a distance. Those who came into these parts on their way to Monte Cassino he asked to take not only of what they heard, but also of what they saw. Because of his love of knowledge, anyone who might unfold something new to him he received without delay, with humility, and chatted with him without awe.

7. Even so he could not learn all the hidden meanings of the Rule. With everyone (not with novices, of course, but with wise persons) he

would make it clear that he learned new and unheard of matters not only from learned people, but also from simpler ones. He caused a book to be compiled from the rules of various fathers, so that blessed Benedict's Rule might be foremost in the minds of all, and gave orders to read it all the time in the morning at assembly. To demonstrate to contentious persons that nothing worthless or useless was set forth by blessed Benedict, but that his Rule was sustained by the rules of others, he compiled another book of statements culled from other rules. To it he gave the title, *Harmony of the Rules*.[123] Statements in agreement with blessed Benedict's book were added to show that the latter was obviously foremost. To it he joined another book from the homilies of holy teachers. These were presented for exhortation of monks and ordered it read all the time at the evening assemblies.

CHAPTER THIRTY-NINE

1. Perceiving that some men panted with all their might to acquire monasteries of monks and strove not only with petitions, but also with money, to obtain them; and that monastic expenses were being sequestered by them for selfish purposes; and that in that way some monasteries were being destroyed and others secured by secular clergy after the monks were driven away, Benedict went to the most pious emperor and pressed him with supplications to ban clergy from contentions of this kind and to set the banished monks free from this danger. The most glorious emperor gave consent and decreed that all monasteries in his realm where there were regular abbots were to be enumerated. By charter he ordered that they remain unchanged for all time and he sealed that charter with his ring. Thus he wiped out the greed of many and at the same time relieved the anxiety of the monks.

2. Certain monasteries were liable to fees and military service. They had as a result reached such dire poverty that the monks lacked both food and clothing. Considering that, the most pious king, at the aforesaid man's suggestion, gave order to relieve them as much as possible so that nothing might be lacking to God's servants. For this relief they gladly prayed to God for the emperor, his children, and the pious establishment of the entire realm. Those monasteries that remained under canonical

123. *Concordia regularum.*

authority he arranged separately so they could live according to the Rule, but the rest he granted to the abbot.

CHAPTER FORTY

What, by God's will, happened once when Benedict was going to a general diet at the emperor's order I think I should not overlook. Although worn by illness and severe fever, he went in obedience to the king's order. Attended only by the weapons of charity, he was prepared to accomplish the benefit of many persons. But the enemy, who always envies holy deeds and seeks to bring detriment to the salvation of pious people, strove by the following craft to slow him down on the path he had taken through vast forests: driving away the horses on which Benedict was traveling, he confused the guides and rendered the way unfamiliar to them. But the man of God was not distressed by grief over the lost horses and he soon reached the royal gates. When the losses to the monasteries and monks were reported to the emperor, he—who had great, constant, and holy solicitude for them—replenished the number of horses. Yet after an interval of a month the lost horses were returned. Thus by divine action it came to pass that Benedict received double reward because he had not grieved over what was lost.

CHAPTER FORTY-ONE

1. Thereafter he began to waste away with various ailments, and with the constant vigils over many years, streaming tears, severe fasts, and prolonged meditations. He undertook, therefore, to prepare his frail, worn body for a new struggle, so that he, who had attained the pinnacle of virtues by subduing vices, might be girded with weapons of patience to strive against infirmities and to gain the victor's double palm from his King after his foes were overthrown. The more vigorously he was mauled by illness, the more intently he persisted over and over again in prayers and readings. No one found him idle, no one found him sluggish at Divine Office, no one found him indulging in vain and frivolous stories.[124] He persisted either in reading by himself or in listening attentively to someone else reading.[125] Who ever found him alone except

---

124. *frivolisque fabulis.* Cf. n. 77 and 38.3 above.
125. Cf. 2.4 above.

weeping?[126] Who ever entered his place unannounced and found his cheeks dry and him not prostrate on the ground or standing with hands outstretched to heaven or catching his tears in his hands lest a page of the sacred volume be stained with them?

2. The powers of his flesh wasted, but his purpose of spirit was firmer than iron. He carried on in the rigor he had begun. Not since the day of his conversion did Benedict eat the flesh of four-footed animals. Even in his last days, when he was worn by listlessness, he scarcely ever indulged in a bath. He was accustomed to change his clothes only after forty days or more.[127] He ordered brothers to read the life and death of the holy fathers to him. Refreshed by that reading his spirit endured even stronger. O good Jesus,[128] his spirit, drenched with sighs and tears, seethed with desire to be released and be with Christ.[129] But he never refused to perform a task if it was helpful to the brothers.

3. As the illness grew stronger, he appealed directly to the emperor to be taken back to his monastery. Delivering a farewell address to the brothers, he spent the whole night in prayers and psalms, then he went to the regular office of that day. On a later day when he completed the regular office and tried to reach the door, a phrase recurred to him, *You are upright, O Lord*.[130] Reciting that versicle, he said, 'I am sinking', and added, *Treat your servant, O Lord, according to your mercy*.[131] Thus amid words of prayer he breathed out his spirit adorned with virtues.

4. His letters, sweeter than all riches, are here. The day before he departed from the world he dictated them with his own mouth to the brothers stationed at Aniane. In them he testified that they would see his face no more.[132] Some declare that at the very hour he departed to Christ, his death was revealed to Bishop Stabilis of Maguelonne. Rising from sleep the latter quickly related to his men what had occurred. We

126. *Gregory the Great*, 29 (Jones, *Saints' Lives*, 117): Gregory entered the church and wept copiously.

127. Cf. 2.4 above.

128. Cf. this exclamation in Paschasius, *Wala*, I. 21.8 (Cabaniss, *Charlemagne's Cousins*, 132).

129. Phil 1:23. *Gregory the Great*, 32 (Hoare, *Western Fathers* 120f.), has the same citation.

130. Ps 119 [118]:137.

131. Ps 119 [118]:124.

132. Acts 20:25, 38.

have touched upon his death cursorily, for brothers who were present at that time have unfolded it more extensively as the following pages indicate.

CHAPTER FORTY-TWO
[From the monks of Inde to Ardo]

1. Abbot Benedict, born in the province of Gothia, lived there from infancy to adolescence in the days of Pepin, king of the Franks, and after his death in the days of his son Charles. Later abandoning the palace, he took the habit of a true monk at the monastery of Saint Seine in the province of Burgundy. There he did battle for God[133] zealously for two and a half years.[134] But because he found little practice of the Rule there, he removed to the regions of Gothia. At first he built, with his own hands, a cell on the river Aniane and afterwards, with the help of brothers who for love of Christ came under his governance, a monastery of new foundation. Not long thereafter he had three hundred monks under his authority.

2. When Emperor Charles died and his son Louis received the empire, the latter caused the venerable man Benedict to come with several followers to Frankland. At first Louis granted Benedict Marmoutier in the countryside of Alsace, but later for love of him erected a completely new monastery for him on the river Inde near the palace of Aix. It was through Benedict that the Lord Christ restored the Rule of Saint Benedict in the entire realm of the Franks. He had under his governance twelve monasteries: Aniane, Gellone, Casa Nova [Goudargues], Ile-Barbe, Ménat, Saint Savinus, Saint Maximin, Massay, Cormery, Celleneuve near Toulouse, Marmoutier in Alsace, and Inde. The last was erected by the emperor's authority for Benedict and his students and endowed from the royal treasuries. For all these Benedict dispatched monks and superiors of his own discipline. He had the greatest concern for the entire ecclesiastical order, whether monks, canons, or layfolk, but especially for monks.

3. The emperor listened to all his advice willingly and accomplished it. For that reason Louis was called by some 'the Monkish'.[135] For love of the holy man he always called the monks 'his own' and after Benedict's decease

133. Cf. note 112 above.
134. See 2.3 and 3.1 above.
135. Probably used only here of Louis.

he went so far as to declare himself openly 'abbot' of this monastery. The holy man continued up to his death in the king's palace for the benefit of all the faithful, although not for earthly profit, because the monastery in which he dwelled was nearby. On the fourth day before his demise[136] and while he was still well, he repeated to the emperor everything that he was in the habit of saying to him. On that day, however, he returned to his own dwelling wracked with fever. On the next day[137] all the emperor's magnates, hearing about it, came to visit him. So great was the throng of bishops, abbots, and monks that we, who were keeping watch over him, scarcely had space to get close to him. Abbot Helisachar came first and remained with him until he died.

4. Benedict grew sicker on the fifth *feria*.[138] On the sixth *feria*[139] at nightfall the emperor sent Tanculf, his chamberlain, ordering that we convey him that very night to the monastery. Lifting him up, we bore him before cock-crow—in company with Helisachar, his men, and ours—to the monastery at the first hour of the day.[140] When the third hour of the day[141] came, Benedict ordered everyone to leave him and he remained alone until the sixth hour.[142] After that Abbot Helisachar and our provost entered and inquired how he was feeling. He replied that he had never been so well and added, 'Until now I have been standing among the choirs of holy ones in the Lord's presence'. On the next day[143] he summoned the brothers, gave them reminders of salvation, then confided to them that in the forty-eight years since he had become a monk he had eaten no food on any day until he had poured out tears before God.

5. On the same day he sent a note of admonition to the emperor and directed others to various monasteries. In them the venerable man noted every office he had performed during the five years and two months before his death, as we found in his records after his death. While still alive he spoke of the offices to be sung for him. He died in his seventies on the third

136. Friday, 8 February 821.
137. Saturday, 9 February.
138. Thursday. Apparently there is either some repetition or discrepancy here.
139. Friday.
140. Prime: the monks are telling time by the 'little hours' of the Divine Office.
141. Terce.
142. Sext.
143. Sunday, 10 February 821.

day before the Ides of February[144] in the year of the Lord's incarnation 821, the fourteenth indiction, first concurrent, fourteenth epact, ninth year[145] of most pious Emperor Louis. We prepared his grave on the third day[146] afterward and put him in a stone coffin that the emperor had had prepared.[147] As we covered his face, we noticed on the forehead, above his eyes, and on his lips a ruddiness such as he never had while alive.

6. These matters having been thus indicated and thus delivered, we, servants of the monastery of Inde, namely, Deidonus, Leovigild, Bertrad, and Desiderius, desire for you, Master Ardo, health in the Lord; and we beg your charity to compose and send to us, according to your God-given wisdom, a little book about the life of our Father Benedict. All of the brothers greet you and do you greet all your brothers for us. Amen.

CHAPTER FORTY-THREE
[From Benedict to George, abbot of Aniane]

1. For George, abbot of the monastery of Aniane, of supreme beatitude and felicity in the Lord Christ, and for all our sons and brothers who live well and watchfully under the standard of Benedict, Benedict, least of all abbots, already at his end, desires health.

2. Above all things and before all matters that burn my spirit and require care is this: that I am intensely solicitous for your order in the regular life. In no way am I unaware that you sweat nobly and are loyally mindful of us and are in no wise wanting in words of encouragement. Set in my last stages, not knowing whether I shall be able to see you again, but since my love turns my spirit toward you, I have taken pains to address to you some words through faithful persons as well as through letters. You know how with all possible labor I have availed as long as I could. Solicitous for you I have exhibited patterns of life and exhortation. Now, therefore, my sons, I pray to God and call Him to witness that you may be of one mind in the

144. Monday, 11 February.
145. Counting from Louis's first coronation in 813.
146. 'On the third day', i.e., two days later, Wednesday, 13 February.
147. Felix, *Saint Guthlac*, 48 (Jones, *Saints' Lives*, 152), Abbess Ecberga, daughter of King Adulf, made for Guthlac a leaden coffin with the request that he be interred in it.

bond of charity[148] and that you may be discreet; that you will not hold as 'foreigners' those whom I have had with me or whom I sent anywhere to set an example or for some reason, and that anyone who may wish to return to you from among them and live with you under the Rule, you will receive in holiness and kindness as brothers, for that is fitting.

3. Thanks to God, material aid will not fail you. To all in general, but especially to those whom you know to be joined with us in friendship, always offer an attentive disposition so far as you can. Minister to poorer monasteries the necessities that are more than sufficient for you. Give aid to Abbot Modan of the monastery of Saint Thibery in those matters in which he may be in want. After my death do even more for these and others than you did in my lifetime. Many monasteries are still corrupt even though they have, through God's largess, received some correction from us. So beware in every way—may it not be, I pray you, merciful Lord—the sinister way . . .[149] that may be able to hold at all times. You at the monastery of Inde, be united as very special brothers.

4. Hold Helisachar (who before others upon earth has always been a loyal friend of canons) and his brothers as in my place and may your refuge be always in him. I am now exhorting you because I do not know whether I shall see you again in this present world. Already on the seventh day before the Ides of February[150] with a very sharp pain, Christ granting His mercy . . .[151] I am stricken. I await nothing other than the last day of my summons speedily.

5. Lord, Benedict ordered the foregoing to be written on the fourth day before the Ides of February[152] while he was still living. He died on the third day before the Ides of the same month.[153]

148. Eph 4:3.
149. Some twenty letters are missing at this point.
150. Thursday, 7 February.
151. Some eight letters are missing.
152. Sunday, 10 February.
153. On 11 February. Here ends the letter.

6.[154]

> The divine seed has been sown;
> may it avail for new ones,
> Drenched with dew from heaven,
> to plow the planting of teachers,
> And the rich field of the heart
> produce fruit a hundredfold.[155]

CHAPTER FORTY-FOUR
[From Benedict to Nibridius]

To Archbishop Nibridius, venerable father in Christ, Abbot Benedict, least of all abbots wishes health and eternal felicity in the Lord. O man of God, may charity, love, and good will now as always move you, by yourself in person or through a servant or friend, to transmit a message throughout all monasteries wherever you can, that they not cease to pour out for me to the Lord prayers, both in psalms and Masses, because they are now profoundly necessary for me. Know, beloved father, that I am now struggling at my end, that my soul has left my body, and that I can no longer see you by the light of the eyes of the body. May He who can make a clean person out of an unclean one, a just person out of a sinner, and a holy one out of an irreligious person, cause us to enjoy the eternal realm there to sing the new song with all the holy ones.[156]

2. I beg, dear father, that as you have always taken an interest in the brothers dwelling at the Aniane monastery, so keep them always more and more in your holy love until your holy soul leaves your body. I commend to you all my friends, servants, and relatives in those areas. In your own monastery, I believe, you work with all your efforts. Be zealous to labor for them with perseverance. Ever use your mouth to all, rich and poor alike, in accord with that statement which the Lord deigned to speak through His blessed apostle Paul: *Declare, implore, scold.*[157] May your holiness know well to whom

---

154. These three hexameters were probably composed by some brother at Inde, not by Ardo.

155. Cf. Mark 4:8.

156. Rev. 14:3.

157. 2 Tim 4:2.

to declare, whom to implore, and whom to scold. I therefore say to you, father, may no peril remain in you whereby you might be forever damned. With free voice may you be able to say with the psalmist, *I have not hidden away your uprightness in my heart, but I have uttered your truth and your salvation.*[158] Do everything, however, with charity and discretion. May the Holy Trinity guard you and grant you bountifully the eternal reward. Amen.

158. Ps 40:10 [39:11].

SHORT INDEX OF NAMES